Recipe for a taste of Magic to last a life time

Ingredients:
- One natural african bush
- A sprinkle of mates
- Various alcoholic beverages
- A few wild animals

Method:
- In a Jacobin, throw the bush and mates together.
- Add a generous helping of alcohol
- Stir
- Add a few wild animals, then more alcohol until you hear some classic chirps
- Then taste and leave to set

Serve the makings of the world's best memories under African skies to the sound of laughter and the call of the wild

home.

FOOD FROM MY KITCHEN

To my family and friends, with you simple food becomes the best kind of feast.

Sarah Graham

A HUGE AND HEARTFELT THANK YOU.

Besides cooking, some of my very favourite moments are spent with Rob, Sophie and our little Isla, who make up our family of four. Without them and the rest of my wonderful family and friends and their endless encouragement, this would all be aimless and empty.

Special thanks to Peter Bhasa, my most able assistant, who patiently, diligently and smilingly helps me every step of the way.

And to my recipe testers and tasters, scattered all around the world, who are all wonderful and amazing and a whole slew of good things in between... and who painstakingly get stuck into a final round of re-testing, tasting and note taking for me, and then send through vital feedback. The deal is that they have to be ruthlessly honest. This time around, they included:

Hilary Barker, Kate Barker, Lucy Bell, Kimbo Brown-Schirato, Debbie Buchner, Kate Chittenden, Wendy Conolly, Tracy Dane, Bronwyn Diering, Ashleigh Graham, Babs Graham, Robyn Graham, Judy Grondel, Teneale Holley, Sarah Hough, Jenna Hutchings, Catherine Lewis, Mandy Liddle, Megan Massingham, Nikki Mullins, Leanne O'Donoghue, Justine Passaportis, Tamryn Paterson, Luciana Popiol, Ruth Tanser, Yvonne Turner, Katherine Tyler, Claire van Tonder, Elsie Velacott, Melanie Watts, Helen Xavier.

Published in 2015 by Struik Lifestyle
(an imprint of Penguin Random House (Pty) Ltd)
Company Reg. No. 1953/000441/07
Estuaries No. 4, Century Avenue (Oxbow Crescent),
Century City, 7441
PO Box 1144, Cape Town 8000, South Africa

Visit **www.randomstruik.co.za** and subscribe to our newsletter for monthly updates and news.

ISBN 978 1 43230 480 5

Publisher: Linda de Villiers
Managing editor: Cecilia Barfield
Editor and indexer: Joy Clack
Designer: Beverley Dodd
Photographer: Warren Heath
Food stylist: Lisa Clark
Food stylist's assistant: Andrea Hirschberg-Dohlhoff
Proofreader: Samantha Fick

Reproduction by Hirt & Carter Cape (Pty) Ltd
Printed and bound by 1010 Printing International Ltd, China

CONTENTS.

INTRODUCTION.

In Swahili, that beautiful lilting language that is native to parts of East Africa, *safari* means 'journey'. And I love that. I love that I have had the privilege of seeing so much of our continent, and the picture it has given me of our food heritage in Africa being such a melting pot of colour and character, food that has been cooked and shared against a beautiful backdrop of lives lived in all its magnificent corners, of stories told, of meals shared around campfires, wood stoves, BBQs (braais) or full and happy tables. And I also love coming home. I love sharing the ideas and inspirations that are gathered along the way.

I grew up in our own little corner of Africa, where my parents have a small game reserve and run a lion conservation project. Where the savanna bends gently against the breeze and the sun seems to shine endlessly out of an enormous blue sky. Responsible tourism has always been at the heart of what my family does, and through it I've been lucky enough to walk with Maasai in remote parts of northern Kenya; feel the exquisite white sand of Zanzibar between my toes; ride elephants and bottle-feed lion cubs in our own backyard; stare in awe at the glory of Table Mountain in the rose-pink light of sunset, and so much in between.

Through our work, there have also been visits to Istanbul, the bright lights of Beijing, New York and so many other special places. With this book, I wanted to share some of that with you, and some of the food that makes these memories come alive. Food that's connected to places that I've been, and places I'd like to go.

What I think I'm trying to say is that this book is about more than just recipes, it's an account of sorts, with heartfelt anecdotes that I hope will keep you company in your own kitchens as you prepare food for feeding the people who you love. It's about our sense of home, with all the splashes of colour that we add to it as we journey through life.

There are, of course, more 'ordinary' dishes that give us a generous helping of simple, uncomplicated everyday food – anyone who knows me knows that I'm all for delicious kitchen quick-fixes and I have never claimed that my food is revolutionary. You will also see my own twists on so many old South African favourites, just their names conjure up an exquisite kaleidoscope of food memories and moments for so many of us: bobotie; snoek; milk tart (*melktert*); malva pudding; chakalaka... And then there are the dishes that take a little longer to coax to glory, but it's so worth making their acquaintance. Those quiet moments at the stove are moments well spent.

So, here's to full and happy tummies and empty plates around merry tables. I hope that you will enjoy this little kitchen companion that is packed full of an abundance of all of the beautiful, simple, honest and sincere recipes that I love to cook; the meals that keep us company as we all meander through our colourful lives.

MY FAVOURITE KITCHEN TIPS AND TRICKS.

With the firm belief that there is no point in reinventing the wheel, these are adapted from *bitten.* (my first book) and then further updated from *smitten.* (my second book), and remain my firm favourites in my little arsenal of kitchen what-to-dos.

Keep it tidy

Clean up as you go along; this means you don't get to the end of the cooking process and your kitchen looks like a bomb went off. I usually keep the bin in the middle of the kitchen floor when I'm cooking more than one thing at a time, so that I can just discard things quickly and easily as I go along. Also, peel vegetables directly over a piece of newspaper for easy cleaning up afterwards.

Act ahead

If we are having people round, I always lay the table before I start cooking. This means that on the odd occasion when you might still be enshrouded in steamy kitchen chaos and hear their knock at the door, it still looks like you're ready for them. It also means that you are not the host who spends most of the evening in the kitchen instead of actually sitting and chatting with your friends.

Well-loved food

Wherever possible, I encourage you to explore where the food you are buying comes from, and to opt for well-loved ingredients. If that means eating fewer, but better quality meat and seafood dishes, then go for it. Try to buy free-range or organic where you can, and also take the time to read more about meat-free Mondays and other tips for how to be 'selective omnivores' on my blog.

Read the recipe!

Always make sure you read the recipe the whole way through before you start cooking. I am a classic culprit for always wanting to get right to the good stuff and have learnt this lesson the hard way!

Get the gear

Being efficient in the kitchen is a whole world easier when you have what you need at your fingertips. This will mean you're more likely to cook and you'll also save money by not eating out or getting take-aways as often. That said, you can very well improvise in a lot of areas, so don't be put off if you don't have some of these things or can't afford them at this stage. Check out my Kitchen Starter Kit on the following page for the basics.

KITCHEN STARTER KIT.

This section is a little companion of convenience as you learn to meander your way through all manner of kitchen paraphernalia.

As well as the usual that you should have lying around the kitchen, here are a few extras that I use regularly when preparing the meals in this book and which I recommend you try to get your hands on at some point. I even think that giving someone this book along with some of the following trinkets is a really fantastic gift idea (of course I do!). All of these items should be easily available at your local supermarket or homeware stores.

Get an oven thermometer

One of the best things I ever did was invest in a nifty little oven thermometer. They are actually reasonably inexpensive and save you a world of pain in the form of burnt or undercooked goodies.

Hand/stick blender

While a proper food processor is amazing if you have one, I often use my faithful stick blender. It liquidises brilliantly and some makes come with a chopper and/or a whisk attachment, which is perfect for finely chopping garlic or ginger, or making pesto and sauces, or whipping cream.

Equipment

Food processor | Electric hand or stand beater | Round and square loose-bottomed baking and fluted tart tins | 12-hole muffin tray | Loaf tin | Quality kitchen scale, preferably electronic | Grater | Small fine grater, for zesting | Set of measuring spoons and measuring cups | 1-litre glass microwave-proof measuring jug | Rolling pin | Pastry brush | Whisk | Kitchen scissors | Assortment of SHARP knives | Wire sieves, large and small | Colander | Good-quality vegetable peeler | Good-quality potato masher | Array of wooden spoons, spatulas and a good ladle

A FEW BASICS.

Use your oven thermometer (see page opposite).

Greasing tins

The easiest method is to take a small square of grease-proof baking paper and a small dollop of butter and work your way around the tin using the paper to hold the butter and smother the surface of the tin gently. I also use baking spray.

Cake testing

A cake is usually done when you insert a skewer or sharp knife and it comes out clean, or if you gently press down on the top with your finger and it 'springs' back out. Don't bother opening your oven to check if something is ready until you can smell it, then you know you're getting close.

What does 'creaming' butter and sugar together mean?

This means beating room temperature butter in a mixing bowl with an electric hand mixer or stand mixer (or a wooden spoon and a lot of elbow grease), and adding in the sugar a little at a time until everything is well blended, fluffy, smooth and 'creamy'.

What on earth is 'blind baking'?

Blind baking means baking a pie or tart crust without the filling so that it firms up, bakes to a light golden colour and doesn't become soggy when you add the filling. As pastry usually shrinks when blind baking, be generous with your pastry. Prick it a good few times with a fork before baking, line loosely with baking paper and a layer of lentils or ceramic baking beads to weigh the pastry down and prevent shrinkage, and bake for 10–15 minutes at 180 °C before removing and allowing to cool to room temperature before filling.

Basic buttercream icing

This can be made easily using a ratio of about 3:1 of sifted icing sugar to butter – e.g. 1 cup icing sugar to $1/3$ cup butter. Blend by adding about 1 Tbsp hot water and flavour as you like with vanilla essence, lemon juice and zest, etc. Beat until extremely light and fluffy.

Resting meat

The difference it makes to any meat – if you give it a chance to rest for 5–10 minutes or longer if it has been slow-roasted and covered loosely with clingfilm or tinfoil – is significant. This ensures the meat remains tender, moist and juicy. Also remember that the meat carries on cooking a little after removing it from the heat and during resting, so if you would like your meat medium-rare, take it off slightly sooner. By the time it's finished resting it should be just right.

CONVERSION TABLE.

Metric	US cups	Imperial
5 ml	1 tsp	1 tsp
15 ml	1 Tbsp	1 Tbsp
60 ml	4 Tbsp ($1/4$ cup)	2 fl oz
80 ml	$1/3$ cup	$2^3/4$ fl oz
125 ml	$1/2$ cup	$4^1/2$ fl oz
160 ml	$2/3$ cup	$5^1/2$ fl oz
200 ml	$3/4$ cup	7 fl oz
250 ml	1 cup	9 fl oz

brunch.

SIMPLE SMOORSNOEK.

SMOORSNOEK IS A TRADITIONAL SOUTH AFRICAN SMOKED FISH DISH, MADE QUITE LIKE A 'HASH' WITH POTATOES, HERBS, FLAKED SMOKED SNOEK AND SOMETIMES CHILLI. SNOEK IS SIMILAR TO MACKEREL/BARACUTA. THIS IS MY OWN RATHER TWISTED TAKE ON IT, BUT IT'S ONE OF MY FAVOURITE WAYS TO START THE DAY. A GOLDEN, GOOEY EGG TOPPING IS NOT AT ALL TRADITIONAL, BUT I LIKE TO THINK THAT IT CROWNS EVERYTHING OFF WITH A PERFECT GOLDEN HALO.

SERVES 4 | PREPARATION TIME 15 minutes | COOKING TIME 20 minutes

WHAT YOU'LL NEED

300 g baby potatoes, quartered
½ cup frozen peas
½ Tbsp butter
½ Tbsp olive oil
1 red onion, chopped
1 cup cherry tomatoes, halved
1 clove garlic, chopped
1 fresh chilli, deseeded and chopped
½ tsp ground cumin
200 g smoked snoek, flaked into pieces and bones removed (or any smoked oily fish)
4–6 eggs (optional)
1 Tbsp chopped fresh dill
1 Tbsp lemon juice and zest of ½ lemon
salt and freshly ground black pepper
fresh crusty bread, for serving

WHAT TO DO

1. Boil the potato quarters in a medium-sized saucepan of salted boiling water for 10 minutes, or until cooked through and they can be pierced easily with a knife. Add the peas for the last 2 minutes of cooking time. Drain and set aside.
2. Heat the butter and olive oil in a heavy-based frying pan on medium-high heat. Fry the onion until translucent, about 5 minutes, then add the tomatoes, garlic, chilli and cumin and cook for another minute. Add the snoek, potatoes and peas to the pan and stir gently until the ingredients are well combined.
3. Remove from the heat and set aside while you quickly poach or fry the eggs (if using).
4. To serve, top each portion with a poached egg, sprinkle over the fresh dill, lemon juice and zest, and a generous pinch of salt and freshly ground black pepper. Serve immediately with slices of fresh crusty bread.

SPICY BAKED BREAKFAST EGGS
with Chorizo and White Beans.

WHEN I FEEL LIKE BRUNCH AROUND A TABLE BRIMMING WITH FRIENDS, THIS IS OFTEN WHAT I FEEL LIKE TUCKING INTO. IT HITS ALL THE RIGHT NOTES FOR LAZY WEEKEND EATING: AN UNDEMANDING ONE-POT WONDER FULL OF BOLD FLAVOURS AND BRIGHT PUNCHES OF FRESHNESS FROM THE HERBS, AND LET'S NOT FORGET THE GORGEOUS STICKY MELTED CHEESE. THERE'S A VERSION OF THIS IN BOTH OF MY PREVIOUS BOOKS TOO – IT'S TOO GOOD TO LEAVE OUT – AND I MAKE IT SO OFTEN THAT THE RECIPE IS CONSTANTLY EVOLVING.

SERVES 6 | PREPARATION TIME 10 minutes | COOKING TIME 35–40 minutes (mostly unattended)
Bake in one medium-sized baking dish or ovenproof pan, or divide into individual ramekins.

WHAT YOU'LL NEED

1 Tbsp olive oil

2 red onions, peeled and roughly chopped

200 g chorizo sausage, or similar, sliced

2 sprigs fresh thyme

1 tsp ground coriander

1 tsp sweet paprika

1 red chilli, deseeded and finely chopped

pinch of salt

1 large red pepper, cored and chopped

2 cups cherry or rosa tomatoes, left whole

1 tsp sugar

1 Tbsp balsamic vinegar

1 clove garlic, crushed

freshly ground black pepper

1 x 410 g can white beans, drained (I use cannellini)

200 g feta or goat's cheese

8–10 eggs

a handful of fresh basil and parsley leaves, for serving

toast or fresh crusty bread, for serving

WHAT TO DO

1. Preheat the oven to 200 °C. Heat the oil in a large pan (preferably ovenproof). Add the onions, sausage, thyme, spices, chilli and salt and fry, over a medium heat, for 5 minutes, or until the onions have softened.
2. Add the red pepper, tomatoes, sugar and vinegar, and cook for another 2–3 minutes, or until the tomatoes are starting to blister. Add the garlic and season with freshly ground black pepper.
3. If your pan is not ovenproof, at this stage transfer the mixture into a large ovenproof dish with a lid (or one that can be covered with tinfoil). Add the beans and crumble over the cheese. Make 8–10 'wells' in the mixture. Break an egg into each well.
4. Cover the dish with the lid or foil and bake for 15–20 minutes, depending on how you like your eggs done. Scatter over the basil and parsley and serve hot, with toast or chunks of fresh crusty bread.

PINEAPPLE, CINNAMON AND GINGER PICKLE.

DELICIOUS SERVED WITH FRESH CRUSTY BREAD AND A SLIVER OR TWO OF STRONG CHEESE.

SERVES 4 | PREPARATION TIME 10 minutes | COOKING TIME 15 minutes

WHAT YOU'LL NEED

1–2 Tbsp cooking oil

1 pineapple, peeled, cored and cut into
   rough cubes

1/2 tsp ground cinnamon

1/4 tsp ground nutmeg

1 Tbsp grated fresh ginger

1 tsp salt

1/2 cup demerara or light brown sugar

100 ml lemon juice

WHAT TO DO

1. Heat the oil in a large heavy-based pan and cook the pineapple until just starting to caramelise.
2. Add the remaining ingredients and simmer for 10–15 minutes, or until the mixture has darkened in colour and thickened slightly.
3. Pour into sterilised jars and allow to cool before sealing. Store in the fridge and, once opened, use within 10 days.

BACON AND CLEMENTINE MARMALADE.

OH GOODNESS. I COULD RAMBLE ON ENDLESSLY ABOUT THE DELICIOUSNESS OF THIS – LET'S JUST SAY THAT IT GENEROUSLY BEFRIENDS EVERYTHING FROM BREAKFAST FRENCH TOAST TO YOUR ULTIMATE HOMEMADE BURGERS AND A WHOLE FEAST OF OPTIONS IN BETWEEN.

SERVES 4 | PREPARATION TIME 5 minutes | COOKING TIME 45 minutes (mostly unattended)

WHAT YOU'LL NEED

250 g lean bacon, diced
1 Tbsp butter
1 Tbsp olive oil
2 red onions, finely diced
3 Tbsp brown sugar
2 Tbsp honey
2 Tbsp brandy
1 tsp grated fresh ginger
$\frac{1}{2}$ vanilla pod
$\frac{1}{2}$ tsp ground cinnamon
$\frac{1}{2}$ tsp ground nutmeg
1 star anise
juice of 1 clementine or orange, and 1 Tbsp
   of the zest

WHAT TO DO

1. Fry the bacon in a frying pan for about 5 minutes, or until golden and crispy. Use a slotted spoon to remove the bacon from the pan and set aside on kitchen paper.
2. Pour out any remaining fat in the pan. Add the butter and olive oil, and then gently fry the onions with the sugar for 7–10 minutes, or until the onions are translucent.
3. Add the remaining ingredients, return the bacon to the pan and simmer gently for about 30 minutes with the lid off. If you find the mixture is becoming too dry, add a little more citrus juice.
4. Allow to cool completely and then store in a sterilised glass jar with a tight-fitting lid. It lasts up to 10 days in the fridge.

CRUSTLESS SPINACH AND SMOKED TROUT QUICHES.

YOU CAN MAKE THESE EITHER IN A CAST-IRON PAN THAT GOES FROM STOVE TO OVEN FOR A REAL ONE-POT WONDER, OR YOU CAN POUR THE FILLING INTO A LIGHTLY GREASED MUFFIN TRAY AND YOU'LL END UP WITH DAINTY LITTLE BREAKFAST BITES THAT ARE HARD NOT TO LOVE. AND IF IT'S BREAKFAST FOR DINNER THAT YOU'RE AFTER, THEN I THINK THIS IS YOUR NUMBER.

SERVES 4–6 | PREPARATION TIME 15 minutes | COOKING TIME 35 minutes

WHAT YOU'LL NEED

FILLING

1 Tbsp olive oil

4 spring onions, chopped

200 g fresh spinach, roughly chopped

100 g smoked trout, roughly chopped

½ cup grated Cheddar cheese

1 Tbsp chopped fresh dill or basil

½ cup crumbled feta or grated
   mozzarella cheese

EGGY CUSTARD

2 eggs

150 ml milk (about ⅔ cup)

pinch of freshly ground black pepper

1 tsp Dijon mustard

WHAT TO DO

1. Preheat the oven to 180 °C and grease a medium-sized pie dish (approximately 20 cm wide) or a muffin tray.
2. Heat the olive oil in a frying pan over medium heat and fry the spring onions for 4–5 minutes, or until they have softened. Add the spinach and stir until it has wilted.
3. Remove the pan from the heat and add the remaining filling ingredients, except the cheese (if you're using a muffin tray, add the cheese too). Stir gently to combine, then spoon this mixture into the pie dish, spreading evenly, and sprinkle over the cheese.
4. Whisk the eggs and milk together. Whisk in the pepper and mustard and pour the egg mixture over the filling. Bake for 25–30 minutes, or until set and lightly golden.

CHOCOLATEY CINNAMON ROLLS.

THESE BEAUTIES, ALONG WITH A CUP OF GOOD COFFEE, ARE ENOUGH TO RESTORE PLEASANTNESS TO ANYONE'S MORNING DISPOSITION.

SERVES 4–6 | PREPARATION TIME 10 minutes | BAKING TIME 15 minutes

WHAT YOU'LL NEED

1 roll ready-made puff pastry, thawed

FILLING

3–4 Tbsp chocolate hazelnut spread

2 Tbsp soft brown sugar

2 tsp ground cinnamon

¼ cup chopped hazelnuts or pecan nuts

¼ cup chocolate chips (optional)

1 Tbsp orange or clementine zest

SUGAR GLAZE

¼ cup buttermilk or soft cream cheese

¼ cup icing sugar

2 Tbsp butter

½ tsp vanilla paste

2 tsp orange or clementine zest

WHAT TO DO

1. Preheat the oven to 240 °C and lightly grease a deep baking tray or muffin tray.
2. Lay out the defrosted puff pastry on a lightly floured surface, and roll out gently until it is about 5 mm thick. Spread the chocolate hazelnut spread over the pastry, then sprinkle over the brown sugar, cinnamon, nuts, chocolate chips (if using) and zest.
3. Starting from the longest edge, roll the dough gently into a 'log' and then cut into 3-cm-thick slices.
4. Lay the slices cut-side up in the baking tray or muffin holes and bake for 15 minutes, or until lightly golden.
5. Remove the rolls and set aside to rest. Meanwhile, prepare the sugar glaze by mixing all the ingredients together and bringing to a gentle simmer in a small saucepan, just until the sugar has dissolved and the ingredients have combined to make a silky mixture, 4–5 minutes. Pour the sugar glaze over the rolls just before serving.

RICOTTA HOTCAKES
with Quick Apple and Vanilla Jam.

READY-IN-A-JIFFY, LIGHT AND FLUFFY AND TOPPED WITH SWEET APPLE AND VANILLA JAM, THESE HOTCAKES ARE REAL CHARMERS.

MAKES about 14 hotcakes | PREPARATION TIME 5 minutes | COOKING TIME 15–20 minutes

WHAT YOU'LL NEED

QUICK APPLE AND VANILLA JAM
2–3 ripe apples, peeled, cored and
    chopped (or pears or nectarines)
1–2 Tbsp honey
1/2 vanilla pod
1 Tbsp lemon juice
1/2 cup water

RICOTTA HOTCAKES
1 cup self-raising flour
1 cup milk
2 Tbsp sugar
1 egg, lightly beaten
1/2 cup ricotta
2 Tbsp butter
2 Tbsp vegetable oil
1/2 cup double-thick Greek yoghurt or
    mascarpone, for serving (optional)

WHAT TO DO

1. Add the jam ingredients to a small saucepan and leave to simmer for 15 minutes, or until the apples have softened and can be mashed easily with a fork. Remove the vanilla pod and set the jam aside to cool.

2. Meanwhile, sift the self-raising flour into a mixing bowl. In a separate bowl, whisk together the milk, sugar, beaten egg and ricotta, and then pour into the flour. Mix gently until combined.

3. Melt 1/2 Tbsp butter and 1/2 Tbsp vegetable oil in a good-quality frying pan on the stove over medium heat, and then dollop in the mixture, about 1/4 cup at a time. You should fit three to four hotcakes in the pan at a time. Cook for 2–3 minutes or until bubbles start to appear on the surface of the hotcakes and the bottoms are golden. Flip and cook for a further 2–3 minutes.

4. Remove the hotcakes and set aside on a plate lined with kitchen paper. Wipe the pan clean with another sheet of kitchen paper. Repeat the cooking process until you have used up all the batter.

5. Serve immediately with the apple and vanilla jam and a dollop of yoghurt or mascarpone if you like.

PUMPKIN FRITTERS
with Preserved Stem-Ginger Cream.

THESE LITTLE WONDERS HAVE THE KNACK OF BEING BOTH LIGHT AND FLUFFY AND RICH AND DECADENT AT THE SAME TIME. THEY'RE A FAVOURITE AT SOUTH AFRICAN TABLES AND IF YOU GIVE THEM A BASH IT WON'T BE DIFFICULT TO SEE WHY. OH, AND THESE ARE CALLED *PAMPOENKOEKIES* IN AFRIKAANS, WHICH SEEMS TO ALLITERATE ALL SORTS OF CUTENESS INTO THEM, DON'T YOU THINK?

SERVES 4–6 | PREPARATION TIME 10 minutes | COOKING TIME 10–15 minutes

WHAT YOU'LL NEED

PRESERVED STEM GINGER CREAM

1–2 Tbsp stem-ginger syrup (or more to taste)

1 tsp finely chopped preserved stem ginger

1 cup double-thick cream, loosened with 1–2 Tbsp milk if necessary

PUMPKIN FRITTERS

500 g pumpkin or butternut squash, peeled and cut into cubes

1 cup self-raising flour

1 tsp baking powder

pinch of salt

1–2 Tbsp sugar

1 egg

¼ cup milk

vegetable oil, for deep frying

zest of 1 orange or lemon

4–6 Tbsp sugar mixed with 1 tsp ground cinnamon, for dusting

WHAT TO DO

1. Mix all the ginger cream ingredients together until smooth. Refrigerate if you're not going to use it right away.
2. Boil the pumpkin or butternut squash until soft and it can be pierced easily with a knife, about 15 minutes. Remove from the heat, drain well and allow to cool completely.
3. Mash the pumpkin or butternut squash and add the flour, baking powder, salt, sugar, egg and milk. Mix until you have a smooth batter. This can be done by hand or in a food processor.
4. Heat the oil in a large heavy-based saucepan over high heat. When the oil is hot (190–200 °C, or when a drop of batter is golden within 30 seconds), carefully drop in spoonfuls of the batter and fry until cooked through and golden, turning to cook both sides evenly. Remove the fritters with a slotted spoon and set aside to drain on kitchen paper. Repeat until you have used all the batter.
5. Mix together the orange or lemon zest and cinnamon sugar and dust each fritter generously before serving immediately with a dollop of the stem-ginger cream.

COCONUT AND PISTACHIO GRANOLA.

THIS GRANOLA CALLS IN THE DAY WITH APLOMB. IT'S JUST A LITTLE SERIOUS, BUT THEN THERE'S THE KICK OF THE SPICES AND THE POP OF SWEETNESS FROM THE CRANBERRIES, AND THE GOLDEN CRUNCH OF THE NUTS, AND IT'S ALL YOU NEED TO GET GOING WITH A SMUG LITTLE SMILE.

MAKES 12 servings | PREPARATION TIME 5 minutes | BAKING TIME 40 minutes (mostly unattended)

WHAT YOU'LL NEED

¼ cup apple juice

¼ cup honey

¼ cup vegetable or coconut oil

2 cups whole rolled oats

1 generous cup of raw roughly chopped almonds, pecans and pistachios (or any nuts of your choice)

¼ cup shredded coconut

1 tsp ground cinnamon

⅓ tsp ground ginger

pinch of ground nutmeg

1 tsp vanilla essence

pinch of salt

½ cup dried cranberries

½ cup dried apricots, roughly chopped (or dried figs!)

WHAT TO DO

1. Preheat the oven to 160 °C and line a baking tray with baking paper.
2. Heat the apple juice, honey and oil together in a small saucepan over low heat until warmed through. Then mix everything, except the dried fruit, together.
3. Spread out on the baking tray and bake for about 40 minutes. After 20 minutes, give it a stir and check that the granola is evenly distributed, and then bake for a further 20 minutes, or until lightly golden and quite brittle.
4. Remove from the oven and let it cool. Break up the granola and add the dried fruit.
5. Store in an airtight container for up to two weeks.

BREAKFAST PLUM PARFAITS.

DON'T PANIC, AND PLEASE DON'T RUN AWAY. A PARFAIT IS NOTHING BUT A FANCY FRENCH WORD FOR A LAYERED DESSERT (USUALLY WITH EGGS AND CREAM INVOLVED). AND THIS IS REALLY ONLY A 'KIND-OF' PARFAIT IN THAT IT'S LAYERED PRETTILY INTO GLASSES WITH LASHINGS OF LUXURIOUS DOUBLE-THICK GREEK YOGHURT (AND IT'S ACTU-ALLY SERVED WITH BREAKFAST IN THIS CASE) AND REALLY REQUIRES NO MORE KITCHEN COMPETENCE THAN USUAL.

SERVES 4 | PREPARATION TIME 10 minutes | COOKING TIME 10 minutes

WHAT YOU'LL NEED

2 cups fresh plum pieces, skin on (alterna-tively use frozen berries)

$\frac{1}{3}$ cup warm water or apple juice

2 Tbsp honey or sugar (or more to taste)

1 tsp clementine or lemon zest

1 cup double-thick Greek yoghurt

$\frac{1}{3}$ cup good-quality granola (or see my recipe opposite)

WHAT TO DO

1. Add the plums, water and honey or sugar to a medium-sized sauce-pan over medium heat and gently simmer until the plums are soft and can be mashed easily with a fork. Stir through the zest and serve once cooled, or store in an airtight container in the fridge for up to five days.

2. To assemble, divide and layer the ingredients as follows into pretty glasses: yoghurt, plum compote, granola, and then serve.

ROSÉ QUINCES.

THERE'S NO WINE INVOLVED HERE (ALTHOUGH A GLASS OR SO OF PINK BUBBLY COULD EASILY REPLACE SOME OF THE POACHING LIQUID AND IT WOULD BE AMAZING); THE ROSÉ ACTUALLY REFERS TO THE BLUSHING RUBY RED OF THE QUINCES AND THEIR SYRUP ONCE THEY HAVE COOKED. REDUCE SOME OF THE SYRUP FURTHER IN A SEPARATE PAN UNTIL IT'S THICK AND GLOSSY AND IT'S AMAZING FOR DRIZZLING OVER EVERYTHING FROM ICE CREAM TO CRUMBLES AND EVEN YOUR BREAKFAST GRANOLA WITH THICK GREEK YOGHURT. YOU CAN ALSO TRY MY RECIPE FOR *PAIN PERDU* (FRENCH TOAST) WITH STICKY SPICED QUINCES (OPPOSITE).

SERVES 4–6 | PREPARATION TIME 10 minutes | COOKING TIME about 1 hour (mostly unattended)

WHAT YOU'LL NEED

6 cups water

150 g sugar

1 Tbsp lemon juice

1 vanilla pod, split lengthways

1 star anise

1 cinnamon stick

4 quinces, just-ripe and fragrant

WHAT TO DO

1. Bring the water to a simmer and add the sugar, lemon juice, vanilla pod, star anise and cinnamon stick.
2. While you heat the water, peel, core and quarter the quinces and then add them to the poaching liquid.
3. Leave to simmer for 45 minutes, or until cooked through and the quinces can be pierced easily with a knife.
4. Store in a sealed container in the fridge for up to seven days.

Note: The quinces and their syrup can also be frozen.

PAIN PERDU
with Greek Yoghurt and Sticky Spiced Quinces.

PAIN PERDU IS JUST THE FRENCH NAME FOR FRENCH TOAST, AND IT TRANSLATES SWEETLY TO 'LOST BREAD', WHICH IS A PRETTY PICTURE TO PAINT OF THE BREAD DUNKED GENEROUSLY IN LIGHTLY WHISKED EGG AND JUST A HINT OF SUGAR BEFORE FRYING. FEEL FREE TO FALL RIGHT IN LOVE.

SERVES 4 | PREPARATION TIME 5–10 minutes | COOKING TIME 10 minutes

WHAT YOU'LL NEED

6 eggs, lightly beaten

½ cup milk

2 Tbsp castor sugar

1 tsp vanilla extract

4 slices bread (ciabatta, sourdough or brioche are best)

1–2 Tbsp cooking oil or butter, for frying

½ cup Greek yoghurt (optional)

1 cup poached quinces with syrup (see Rosé Quinces, opposite)

WHAT TO DO

1. Whisk together the eggs, milk, castor sugar and vanilla until light and fluffy, no more than 30 seconds.
2. Soak the bread slices in the egg mixture for 1–2 minutes.
3. Add the oil to a large pan over medium-high heat and then fry your eggy bread slices for 2–3 mintues on each side, or until golden.
4. Serve immediately with a spoonful of Greek yoghurt (if using) and two to three slices of poached quinces along with a drizzle of the sticky syrup.

Note: If quinces are not available, use canned guavas or figs in their syrup and warm in a small saucepan before serving.

BEAUTIFUL QUINOA BREKKIE BOWLS.

YOU MIGHT THINK THAT IT'S A LITTLE EXTRAVAGANT TO USE QUINOA THIS WAY, BUT TO ME IT'S MONEY WELL SPENT TO KICK OFF YOUR DAY WITH SUCH A PERFECTLY DELICIOUS LITTLE NUMBER.

SERVES 4 | PREPARATION TIME 10 minutes | COOKING TIME 15–20 minutes

WHAT YOU'LL NEED
¾ cup quinoa, cooked according to
    packet instructions
2 tsp light brown sugar or honey
½ tsp ground cinnamon
1 cup mixed berries, preferably fresh
1 cup natural yoghurt
¼ cup raw oats (or muesli or granola
    of your choice)
½ cup mixed toasted nuts
¼ cup runny honey
small handful roasted pumpkin seeds
coconut shavings

WHAT TO DO
1. Cook the quinoa according to the packet instructions, using milk (or almond milk) instead of water, and adding in the 2 tsp brown sugar or honey for a little sweetness, along with the ground cinnamon. Add a little hot water as it cooks if you find that it becomes too thick, although you are looking for a porridgy consistency.
2. When the quinoa is cooked, layer your breakfast into small glass jars or bowls, dividing the remaining ingredients between them.

GRAPEFRUIT AND STAR ANISE LEMONADE.

A GLASS FULL OF THIS WITH LOTS OF CLINKING ICE IS WHO YOU WANT TO BE FRIENDS WITH ON A SUN-KISSED SUMMERY DAY. IT'S GOT JUST THE RIGHT NOTES OF SHARPNESS AND SPICE TO KEEP THINGS LIVELY.

SERVES 4 | PREPARATION TIME 40 minutes (mostly unattended)

WHAT YOU'LL NEED

zest of 1 grapefruit
juice of 3 grapefruit
juice of 2 lemons
½ cup water
⅓ cup light brown sugar or honey
2 star anise
1 cinnamon stick
1 vanilla pod, halved lengthways

WHAT TO DO

1. Add all of the ingredients to a heavy-based saucepan and simmer gently until the sugar has dissolved and the mixture has thickened to a syrupy consistency, 30–40 minutes. Set aside and allow to cool completely.
2. To serve, strain the grapefruit syrup and dilute to taste with soda water, ginger ale or lemonade, or a mixture of these.
3. Keep refrigerated and use within 10 days.

Note: Make this a little more grown-up by adding a dash or two of gin.

salads.

BARLEY, SPINACH AND WILD MUSHROOM SALAD
with Balsamic Dressing.

I LOVE THE AL DENTE NUTTINESS OF THE BARLEY, AND THE COMBINATION WITH THE SPINACH AND WILD MUSH-ROOMS IS EARTHY AND FRESH AND JUST LOVELY. IF YOU PREFER, YOU CAN USE QUINOA, WILD RICE OR CHICKPEAS.

SERVES 4 | PREPARATION TIME 10–15 minutes | COOKING TIME 15 minutes

WHAT YOU'LL NEED

BALSAMIC DRESSING

3 Tbsp olive oil

2 Tbsp lemon juice

1 Tbsp balsamic vinegar

2 tsp runny honey

1 fresh red chilli, deseeded and finely
  chopped (optional)

SALAD

1 cup pearled barley

3 Tbsp olive oil

2 tsp honey

1 Tbsp butter

250 g mixed wild mushrooms, chopped

1 clove garlic, minced

1 Tbsp balsamic vinegar

100 g baby spinach leaves, rinsed

100 g feta cheese

squeeze of lemon juice, or more to taste

zest of ½ lemon

1 Tbsp each chopped mint, basil and parsley

salt and freshly ground black pepper

WHAT TO DO

1. Prepare the balsamic dressing by shaking all the ingredients together in a small jam jar. It's a good idea to double the recipe to have extra for use later in the week. Taste and check for seasoning before serving.

2. Cook the barley according to the packet instructions. Drain and allow to cool before mixing through the 2 Tbsp of the olive oil and the honey. Tip into a serving bowl.

3. To a large heavy-based pan over medium-high heat, add the remaining 1 Tbsp olive oil and the butter. When the butter starts to foam, add the mushrooms and fry for 2–3 minutes, then add the garlic and cook for another minute. Add the balsamic vinegar and simmer gently for a further minute or two before adding the spinach leaves. Remove the pan from the heat, and stir gently until the spinach leaves have wilted. Gently spoon these ingredients over the barley in the serving bowl.

4. Crumble over the feta and add the lemon zest and juice and fresh herbs, as well as a sprinkling of salt and pepper. Drizzle over half the dressing and serve immediately with the remaining dressing on the side.

WARM TOMATO AND BARLEY SALAD
with Mint, Basil and Goat's Cheese.

BARLEY AGAIN. BUT IT'S HARD NOT TO. IT'S A FIRM FAVOURITE AT OUR TABLE; BARLEY IS A VERY HUMBLE BLANK CANVAS TO SO MANY DIFFERENT FLAVOURS AND IS ALSO REALLY BUDGET-FRIENDLY.

SERVES 4 | PREPARATION TIME 10 minutes | COOKING TIME 25–30 minutes

WHAT YOU'LL NEED

SALAD
1 cup pearled barley

1 Tbsp olive oil

1 heaped cup chopped ripe tomatoes

1 Tbsp each chopped fresh parsley, mint and basil

100 g goat's cheese, roughly crumbled

zest of 1 lemon

DRESSING
3 Tbsp lemon juice

5 Tbsp olive oil

1–2 Tbsp honey

1 tsp Dijon mustard (optional)

generous pinch each of salt and freshly ground black pepper

WHAT TO DO

1. Cook the barley according to packet instructions, drain, drizzle with the olive oil and tip into a serving bowl.
2. Meanwhile, prepare the salad dressing by shaking all the ingredients together in an old jam jar. Check for seasoning.
3. In a serving bowl, gently toss together the barley, tomatoes and herbs and scatter over the goat's cheese and lemon zest. Drizzle over the dressing, check for seasoning and serve.

ROASTED CORN AND CHICKPEA SALAD.

I'M ALMOST NEVER WITHOUT A CAN OF CHICKPEAS IN MY PANTRY. THEY ARE ENDLESSLY WELCOMING TO SO MANY OTHER FLAVOURS. HERE, I'VE ADDED BEAUTIFUL GOLDEN NUGGETS OF BLISTERED CORN TO A SIMPLE, HERBY CHICK-PEA SALAD AND THE RESULT IS PRETTY AMAZING.

SERVES 4–6 | PREPARATION TIME 10 minutes | COOKING TIME 30 minutes

WHAT YOU'LL NEED

DRESSING

2 Tbsp olive oil

juice of 1 lemon or 2–3 Tbsp red
  wine vinegar

1–2 tsp Dijon mustard

1 Tbsp honey

1 small chilli, deseeded and finely
  chopped (optional)

pinch of salt and freshly ground
  black pepper

SALAD

3–4 fresh whole corn on the cob

1 Tbsp olive oil

½ tsp ground cumin

½ tsp ground coriander

2 x 410 g cans chickpeas, drained

½ red onion, finely chopped

75 g feta or soft goat's cheese,
  roughly crumbled

1 Tbsp chopped fresh coriander,
  mint or basil

salt and freshly ground black pepper

WHAT TO DO

1. Mix all the dressing ingredients together in a jar until the dressing emulsifies, then check for seasoning and balance of flavours.
2. Drizzle the corn with the olive oil and grill until blistered and golden. Allow to cool for a few minutes and then slice off the kernels.
3. Mix the corn kernels with the spices, chickpeas, onion and cheese and tip out onto a serving platter. Stir through the herbs and dressing. Season well with salt and pepper.

AUBERGINE, PINE NUT AND LABNEH SALAD.

By Ishay Govender-Ypma, FoodAndTheFabulous Blog.

ISHAY (MY BEAUTIFUL, EXOTIC, INTELLIGENT LAWYER TURNED FOOD AND TRAVEL WRITING FRIEND) AND I COOKED THIS TOGETHER IN EPISODE 9 OF *SARAH GRAHAM COOKS CAPE TOWN*, WHEN SHE SO KINDLY INVITED US TO FEAST WITH HER AT HOME. IT'S BECOME ONE OF MY FAVOURITE WAYS TO USE BEAUTIFULLY PLUMP PURPLE AUBERGINES. LABNEH IS A VERY SOFT CHEESE MADE FROM STRAINED YOGHURT, AND IT'S AMAZING. IT'S ALSO REALLY EASY TO MAKE AT HOME – STRAIN 2 CUPS LIGHTLY SALTED THICK NATURAL YOGHURT THROUGH A CHEESECLOTH-LINED SIEVE SET OVER A CLEAN BOWL IN THE FRIDGE FOR ABOUT TWO DAYS, SQUEEZE OUT ANY EXCESS LIQUID AND ROLL INTO SMALL BALLS. ADD TO A CLEAN JAR ALONG WITH ENOUGH OLIVE OIL TO COVER, AND A SMALL HANDFUL OF CHOPPED FRESH HERBS AND LEMON ZEST, AS WELL AS CHILLIES OR GARLIC. ALTERNATIVELY, DON'T ROLL INTO BALLS AND JUST STIR THROUGH THE HERBS, LEMON, ETC. AND SERVE AS A DELICIOUS DIP OR SPREAD.

SERVES 4 | PREPARATION TIME 10–15 minutes | COOKING TIME 35–45 minutes

WHAT YOU'LL NEED

2 large aubergines

1 Tbsp dried chilli flakes

2 Tbsp sumac

sea salt flakes and freshly ground
  black pepper

olive oil

2 Tbsp pine nuts, toasted until lightly
  golden and fragrant

about 20 mint leaves, rinsed

zest of 1 lemon

10 small labneh balls (or ricotta)

DRESSING

pomegranate molasses

pomegranate seeds (arils), for garnishing

WHAT TO DO

1. Preheat the oven to 180 °C.
2. Slice the aubergines into discs, about 1 cm thick.
3. Season with the chilli, sumac, salt and pepper and olive oil and lay them flat on a baking tray.
4. Roast for 35–45 minutes or until cooked through and golden. Remove from the oven and lay out on a platter to cool slightly.
5. Top with the toasted pine nuts, mint leaves, lemon zest, labneh or ricotta and a drizzle of pomegranate molasses. Finish off with a scattering of pomegranate seeds and serve immediately.

RED QUINOA, PEAR AND GORGONZOLA SALAD.

THIS SALAD IS JUST A LITTLE GOURMET, BUT WITHOUT BEING STUCK-UP OR STUFFY. THE DUSTY RED OF THE QUINOA ADDS A LITTLE SOMETHING SPECIAL, AND I LIKE TO THINK THAT THE ROASTED PEAR AND GORGONZOLA ROUND THINGS OFF RATHER NICELY.

SERVES 4 | PREPARATION TIME 10 minutes | COOKING TIME 15 minutes

WHAT YOU'LL NEED

1 cup red quinoa

1½ cups water (or amount as given
  on the packet)

3 ripe pears, cored and cut into
  rough chunks

1 Tbsp melted butter or olive oil

1 Tbsp olive oil

1 Tbsp lemon juice

handful fresh rocket or baby spinach
  leaves, rinsed

100 g Gorgonzola

salt and freshly ground black pepper

WHAT TO DO

1. Preheat the oven to 220 °C.
2. Using a fine-meshed sieve, rinse the quinoa thoroughly under cool running water. Then, to a medium-sized saucepan, add the quinoa along with the water. Turn the heat to high, bring the water to a boil, then place the lid on the pot, turn down to a gentle simmer and cook for a further 10 minutes or until no water remains. Leave to rest with the lid on. This steaming further dries out the quinoa as it steams, ensuring a fluffy result.
3. Meanwhile, place the pears into an ovenproof dish, brush with the melted butter or olive oil and roast for 5–10 minutes, or until golden.
4. To serve, drizzle the olive oil and lemon juice over the quinoa and toss through the rocket or spinach leaves. Scatter over the pear pieces and crumble over the Gorgonzola before serving. Season to taste.

CRISPY SQUID, CHICKPEA AND CHORIZO SALAD
with Lemony Mustard Dressing.

THIS SALAD HAS BOTH PRETTINESS AND PUNCH, ONE OF MY FAVOURITE COMBINATIONS. IT'S BOLD AND FULL OF FLAVOUR BUT STILL LIGHT AND FRESH. I ALWAYS THINK OF IT AS A REAL HEAD-TURNING CROWD PLEASER. I HOPE YOU WILL TOO.

SERVES 4 | PREPARATION TIME 5–10 minutes | COOKING TIME 10 minutes

WHAT YOU'LL NEED

LEMONY MUSTARD DRESSING

3 Tbsp olive oil

2 Tbsp lemon juice or red wine vinegar

2 tsp runny honey

1 tsp Dijon mustard

1 fresh red chilli, deseeded and finely
  chopped (optional)

SALAD

1 Tbsp olive oil

150 g chorizo, roughly chopped

400 g squid, cleaned and cut into rings

small handful each roughly torn fresh mint,
  basil and parsley

100 g cherry or rosa tomatoes, halved at
  varying angles

1 x 410 g can chickpeas, drained

50 g feta cheese

WHAT TO DO

1. Shake all the dressing ingredients together in an old jam jar, then check for seasoning.
2. Add the oil to a heavy-based pan over medium-high heat and then fry the chorizo for 3–4 minutes until lightly golden. Remove and set aside to drain on kitchen paper.
3. Add the squid to the same pan that you used to fry the chorizo, and fry until crispy and golden, about 3 minutes. Remove and set aside with the chorizo.
4. To assemble the salad, add the chorizo, squid, herbs, tomatoes and chickpeas to a bowl, toss gently and then top with the feta cheese.
5. Drizzle over the salad dressing and serve immediately, or set aside and dress just before serving.

ROASTED BEETROOT AND LENTIL SALAD
with Herbed Yoghurt Dressing.

I LOVE THE DEEP EARTHINESS OF BOTH LENTILS AND BUTTERNUT – AND TOSSED TOGETHER HERE WITH A HINT OF MIDDLE EASTERN SPICE, A POP OF COLOUR FROM THE FRESH HERBS AND CRUMBLED GOAT'S CHEESE, IT'S PRETTY AS A PICTURE.

SERVES 2 | PREPARATION TIME 10 minutes | COOKING TIME 30 minutes (mostly unattended)

WHAT YOU'LL NEED

750 g fresh whole beetroot
1–2 Tbsp olive oil
$\frac{1}{2}$ tsp ground cumin
$\frac{1}{2}$ tsp ground coriander
1 x 400 g can lentils in water, drained
$\frac{1}{2}$ red onion, finely chopped
1 Tbsp each chopped fresh mint and
    parsley (or coriander)
75 g feta or goat's cheese
salt and freshly ground black pepper

HERBED YOGHURT DRESSING

$\frac{1}{2}$ cup natural yoghurt
1 Tbsp olive oil
1 Tbsp chopped fresh parsley
1 Tbsp chopped fresh mint or basil
1 tsp lemon zest
1 Tbsp lemon juice
salt and freshly ground black pepper

WHAT TO DO

1. Preheat the oven to 200 °C.
2. Cook the beetroot in a saucepan of salted boiling water until soft and then drain, peel and roughly chop (if you like, use kitchen gloves for the peeling part to avoid staining your hands pink).
3. Using a large baking tray, toss the beetroot with the olive oil and spices until coated, and then roast on the middle shelf for about 15 minutes.
4. Add the warm beetroot to a serving bowl along with the lentils and red onion. Stir in the fresh herbs. Crumble over the cheese, drizzle over a little more olive oil and season well with salt and pepper.
5. Mix together the dressing ingredients and serve alongside the salad. Alternatively, serve with a lighter, sharper Lemony Mustard Dressing (see page 37), or you could serve both.

Notes: For a speedier version, use precooked beetroot, but not the kind stored in vinegar.
If available, add generous chunks of fresh avocado for a little extra creaminess and colour.

COURGETTE RIBBON AND BROAD BEAN SALAD
with Pecorino and Mint.

SPRING! I LOVE THE BURST OF BRIGHT GREENNESS AND THE TINIEST SUNNY SPRINKLING OF FRESH LEMON ZEST. ALSO, THIS IS JUST AS AT HOME AS IT IS, OR DRAPED HAPPILY OVER FRESH PASTA OR TUCKED INTO A STEAMING BOWL OF WARM QUINOA OR COUSCOUS.

SERVES 4 | PREPARATION TIME 5 minutes | COOKING TIME 5 minutes

---

WHAT YOU'LL NEED

1 Tbsp olive oil

200 g courgettes, trimmed and sliced into ribbons with a vegetable peeler

1 cup shelled broad beans

1 cup frozen peas, thawed

salt and freshly ground black pepper

1 Tbsp olive oil

1 Tbsp lemon juice

1 tsp lemon zest

small handful fresh mint leaves, torn

handful pecorino or Parmesan shavings

WHAT TO DO

1. Add the olive oil to a medium-sized pan over medium-high heat and fry the courgette ribbons until lightly golden. Remove and set aside on kitchen paper to drain.
2. Meanwhile, boil the broad beans and peas for 1 minute in lightly salted water. Drain and set aside.
3. Lay the courgettes on a small serving platter, add the broad beans and peas and season lightly with salt and pepper. Add the olive oil, lemon juice and zest. Sprinkle over the mint leaves and pecorino or Parmesan shavings and serve immediately.

STICKY GINGER PRAWN SALAD.

THIS IS FRESH AND FEISTY AND PRETTY AND ZINGY AND HEALTHY AND ALTOGETHER FAB.

SERVES 4 | PREPARATION TIME 10 minutes | COOKING TIME 10 minutes

WHAT YOU'LL NEED

PRAWNS

1 Tbsp cooking oil

20–25 prawns, deveined and peeled

1 small clove garlic, minced

2 Tbsp honey

2 Tbsp soy sauce

1 heaped tsp grated fresh ginger

1–2 tsp fish sauce

2 Tbsp lime juice

SALAD

½ cucumber, deseeded and grated

2 medium carrots, grated

2 pears, grated, or use raw beetroot

1 avocado, depipped, peeled and roughly
   cut into cubes

handful fresh sprouts

handful salted peanuts

1 Tbsp each chopped fresh mint and basil
   (or coriander)

WHAT TO DO

1. Add the oil to a large frying pan over medium-high heat and fry the prawns until just pink and cooked through. Add the garlic and cook for another minute. Remove from the heat, add the remaining ingredients for the prawns and toss until warmed through. Set aside.

2. Prepare the salad ingredients, gently squeeze the cucumber to remove any excess water, and add everything to a large serving bowl.

3. Add the prawns to the salad and drizzle over any excess pan juices. Serve immediately.

Notes: If using grated pear, I suggest drizzling it with a little lemon juice after grating to prevent browning.
You can also add raw roughly broken two-minute noodles for a little extra crunch if you like.

BLISTERED NECTARINE, BACON AND BURRATA SALAD
with Watercress Pesto Dressing.

THIS SALAD SEEMS TO EXPLODE ONTO THE PLATE IN A RIOT OF COLOUR AND FLAVOURS AND TEXTURES, AND CAPTURES THE VERY ESSENCE OF SUMMER. IT'S BEAUTIFUL TO LOOK AT AND BEAUTIFUL TO EAT.

SERVES 4 | PREPARATION TIME 20 minutes | COOKING TIME 10 minutes

WHAT YOU'LL NEED

WATERCRESS PESTO DRESSING

50 g fresh watercress, rinsed and largest
   stalks removed

2 Tbsp blanched almonds

4 Tbsp olive oil

2 Tbsp lemon juice

1 tsp lemon zest

$1/4$–$1/2$ tsp sugar, or more to taste

pinch of salt and freshly ground
   black pepper

2 Tbsp warm water, to loosen

SALAD

4 ripe nectarines, stones removed and
   sliced into wedges

olive oil, for brushing

$1/4$ cup roughly chopped pecan nuts
   or walnuts

200 g bacon, diced

50 g mixed salad leaves, rinsed

200 g burrata mozzarella balls, roughly torn
   (or feta, Gorgonzola or goat's cheese)

WHAT TO DO

1. Preheat the oven grill.
2. Blend all the dressing ingredients together and check for seasoning.
3. Place the nectarine wedges cut-side up in an ovenproof dish, brush with olive oil and grill for 5 minutes, or until just starting to blister.
4. In a small dry frying pan on the stovetop, toast the nuts over medium-high heat until just lightly golden, stirring from time to time. Remove and set aside to cool.
5. Fry the bacon in the pan that you used for the nuts over medium-high heat until crispy, then remove and set aside on kitchen paper.
6. Remove the nectarines from the oven and allow to cool for a few minutes, then gently layer them over the salad leaves. Add the cheese, toasted nuts and bacon, then squeeze over a little extra lemon juice.
7. Serve with the watercress pesto dressing on the side.

Note: For a speedier salad dressing, simply drizzle with olive oil and a squeeze of lemon juice or balsamic vinegar.

soups.

FIERY LENTIL AND CHORIZO SOUP.

THIS SOUP IS COSY AND FULL OF CHARACTER; IT'S YOUR BEST MATE ON A CHILLY WINTERY EVENING WHEN YOU WANT TO BE CURLED UP SOMEWHERE WARM AND COMFY.

SERVES 2 | PREPARATION TIME 5–10 minutes | COOKING TIME 15 minutes

WHAT YOU'LL NEED

1–2 Tbsp olive oil
1 red onion, chopped
1–2 tsp harissa paste (or to taste) (alternatively, use 1 tsp dried chilli flakes)
200 g chorizo sausage, roughly chopped
1 clove garlic, minced
1 x 410 g tin peeled, chopped tomatoes
2 cups chicken or vegetable stock
1 tsp sugar
1 x 400 g tin lentils, drained
salt and freshly ground black pepper
1 Tbsp each roughly chopped fresh basil and parsley, for serving
crumbled feta cheese, for serving (optional)

WHAT TO DO

1. Add the olive oil to a pan on medium-high heat and fry the onion for about 5 minutes, or until softened, stirring occasionally.
2. Add the harissa paste and chorizo and cook for 2–3 minutes. Add the garlic and tomatoes and cook for another minute, then add the stock and sugar. Leave to simmer for another 10 minutes.
3. Add the lentils and stir until heated through. Remove from the heat and serve immediately in warmed bowls with a sprinkling of fresh herbs and feta cheese (if using). You can also serve toasted pita breads or any fresh crusty bread on the side.

SPICY SPLIT PEA SOUP.

WHEN THE FIRST CHILL OF AUTUMN HITS THE AIR, HEAD ON OVER TO YOUR KITCHEN AND RUSTLE UP A POT OF THIS OH-SO-HEARTWARMING SPLIT PEA SOUP. IT'S TOTALLY UNFUSSY AND WILL BUBBLE AWAY MERRILY WHILE YOU PUT YOUR FEET UP. *LEKKER NÈ?*

SERVES 4 | PREPARATION TIME 5–10 minutes | COOKING TIME approx. 1½ hours (mostly unattended)

WHAT YOU'LL NEED

1 Tbsp olive oil
1 medium-sized onion, chopped
1 tsp ground cumin
1 tsp ground coriander
pinch of ground cinnamon
½ tsp dried chilli flakes
1 heaped tsp grated fresh ginger
1 clove garlic, crushed
6 cups (1.5 L) chicken stock
500 g yellow split peas, rinsed
salt and freshly ground black pepper
   to taste
sugar to taste
lemon juice to taste
fresh coriander leaves, for garnishing
fresh crusty bread, for serving

WHAT TO DO

1. In a large saucepan, heat the olive oil over medium-high heat and fry the onion, spices and ginger until the onion has softened but not coloured, about 5 minutes. Add the garlic and fry for another minute.
2. Add the chicken stock and the split peas, stir and leave to simmer gently, covered, for 1½ hours, or until the split peas are cooked through. Add a little extra water to the soup if it becomes too thick during the cooking process.
3. Add salt, pepper, sugar and lemon juice to taste. Remove from the heat and blend to your desired consistency, loosening with hot water if necessary. Serve with a drizzle of olive oil, fresh coriander leaves and fresh crusty bread.

ROAST CHICKEN AND FENNEL SOUP.

THIS IS OUR GO-TO WEEKNIGHT SOUP, AND IT NEVER GETS OLD. IT'S AS BEGUILING ON A CHILLY WINTER'S NIGHT AS IT IS ON GLORIOUSLY SUNNY SUMMER DAYS. IT'S ALSO YOUR LEFTOVER ROAST CHICKEN'S NEW BEST FRIEND.

SERVES 4 | PREPARATION TIME 15 minutes | COOKING TIME 20 minutes

WHAT YOU'LL NEED

1 Tbsp olive oil

1 medium-sized onion, chopped

3–4 baby leeks, chopped

1 cup chopped celery

1 medium-sized fennel bulb, chopped

4 cups (1 L) good-quality chicken stock

1 leftover roast chicken carcass

about 1 cup leftover roast chicken meat

salt and freshly ground black pepper

2 Tbsp torn fresh parsley or basil,
    for serving

1 tsp lemon zest, for serving

WHAT TO DO

1. Heat the olive oil in a large saucepan over medium heat and fry the onion and leeks for 7–10 minutes, or until softened.
2. Add the celery and fennel and cook for another 3–4 minutes; you want them to retain a little crunch.
3. Add the chicken stock, chicken carcass and meat and simmer for a further 10 minutes. Remove from the heat and carefully remove the chicken carcass and any other bones. Season to taste.
4. Serve in warmed bowls with a scattering of fresh herbs and some lemon zest.

Notes: For a bulkier version, add ½ cup pearled barley and leave to simmer a little longer, until the barley is cooked but still slightly al dente. You can blend this soup until smooth, although I prefer the broth-style. This soup freezes for up to two months.

QUICK THAI NOODLE SOUP
with Chicken Dumplings.

SERVES 4 | PREPARATION TIME 10 minutes | COOKING TIME 15–20 minutes (plus fridge resting time for dumplings, 30 minutes or up to 1 day in advance)

WHAT YOU'LL NEED

DUMPLINGS
300 g chicken mince

1 tsp Chinese five-spice

1 spring onion, finely chopped

1 heaped tsp grated fresh ginger

1 chilli, deseeded and finely chopped

1 Tbsp chopped fresh coriander or basil

1 tsp fish sauce

1 Tbsp lemon or lime juice

1 egg or 1–2 Tbsp cornflour, for binding

pinch of freshly ground black pepper

SOUP
1 Tbsp olive oil

1 heaped Tbsp Thai red curry paste

1 heaped tsp grated fresh ginger

1 clove garlic, minced

6 cups (1.5 L) chicken or vegetable stock

200 g egg noodles (optional)

1 red pepper, deseeded and thinly sliced

100 g sugar snap peas, halved lengthways

100 g baby pak choi, halved lengthways

1 Tbsp fish sauce, or more to taste

1 tsp sugar, or more to taste

juice of 1 lime, or more to taste

handful fresh coriander or Thai basil,
   roughly chopped, for garnishing

WHAT TO DO

1. To make the dumplings, combine all the ingredients in a large bowl. With slightly wet hands, roll into golf ball-sized rounds and set aside on a clean plate in the fridge to firm up for at least 30 minutes.
2. Heat the olive oil in a large pot over medium-high heat and fry the curry paste for 2 minutes until fragrant. Add the ginger and garlic, and fry for another minute, then add the stock and bring to a boil.
3. Turn down the heat to medium-low and add the chicken dumplings. The liquid should not be bubbling too vigorously at this stage as the dumplings might break apart. Leave the dumplings to poach in the liquid for 6–8 minutes, or until cooked through.
4. Add the remaining soup ingredients up to and including the sugar and cook for a further 1–2 minutes.
5. Remove the saucepan from the heat, stir in the lime juice, check for seasoning and balance of flavours, adjust where necessary and serve immediately in warmed bowls, garnished with a sprinkling of fresh coriander or Thai basil.

Notes: For a speedier version, you can leave out the dumplings and just poach chicken breast fillet strips directly in the soup for 5–7 minutes before adding the vegetables and serving.

Add more or less Thai red curry paste, according to taste and brand.

Use 4 cups (1 L) stock and 1 x 410 ml can coconut milk for a creamier version of this soup.

ROASTED BUTTERNUT AND PEAR SOUP
with Candied Bacon Croutons.

I KNOW, BUTTERNUT SOUP. THIS COULD VERY POSSIBLY BE UNDERWHELMING. BUT HERE, THE PEAR ADDS A LOVELY SWEET FRESHNESS AND LIGHTNESS, AND THE SPICES BRING ANOTHER LEVEL OF FLAVOUR THAT I ALWAYS GET EXCITED ABOUT. OH, AND LET'S NOT FORGET THOSE EXQUISITE LITTLE BITS OF STICKY MAPLE SYRUP BACON THAT WE'RE SCATTERING OVER THE TOP.

SERVES 3–4 | PREPARATION TIME 10 minutes | COOKING TIME 1 hour (mostly unattended)

WHAT YOU'LL NEED
900 g butternut, peeled and cubed (it's a good idea to buy ready-peeled and cubed in this case)
1 medium onion, roughly chopped
1 Tbsp olive oil
½ tsp ground cinnamon
¼ tsp ground nutmeg
½ tsp ground coriander (you could also use cumin)
1 fresh chilli, deseeded and chopped (optional)
salt and freshly ground black pepper
2 pears, peeled, cored and roughly chopped
about 3 cups chicken stock made with just-boiled water

BACON CROUTONS
1 Tbsp olive oil
3–4 rashers bacon, roughly chopped
1–2 Tbsp maple syrup
fresh crusty bread for serving

WHAT TO DO
1. Preheat the oven to 180 °C.
2. Drizzle the butternut cubes and onion with the olive oil, sprinkle over the spices and chilli, season lightly with salt and pepper and roast until lightly golden and the butternut has cooked through, about 45 minutes. Add the pear pieces about halfway through so that they don't burn.
3. Add the butternut, onion and pears to a blender and pour in the hot stock, starting with 2 cups. Blend until smooth, adding the final cup if necessary, depending on your preferred consistency. Season to taste and set aside until serving.
4. Meanwhile, heat the olive oil in a frying pan until very hot. Fry the bacon bits until crispy, pour out any excess oil, then pour over the maple syrup, remove from the heat and set aside until serving.
5. Scatter the crispy maple bacon over the soup before serving in warmed bowls with fresh crusty bread on the side.

Note: This soup freezes well for up to two months.

ARRABBIATTA SEAFOOD SOUP
with Parmesan Ciabatta Toasts.

YUM. I LOVE THE HIT OF CHILLI THAT COMES WITH AN ARABIATTA SAUCE (IT TRANSLATES TO 'ANGRY' IN ITALIAN). I ALSO THINK THIS SAUCE IS A BRILLIANT WAY TO MAKE THE SEAFOOD SHINE.

SERVES 4 | PREPARATION TIME 5–10 minutes | COOKING TIME 25 minutes

WHAT YOU'LL NEED

1 Tbsp olive oil

1 clove garlic, finely chopped

1 fresh red chilli, deseeded and finely chopped or ½ tsp dried chilli flakes

2 x 410 g cans peeled, chopped tomatoes

2 sprigs fresh thyme or ½ tsp dried

1 tsp sugar

1 cup fish or vegetable stock

400 g firm white fish fillets, without skin, cut into 2 cm cubes

750 g fresh mussels with shells intact and rinsed

400 g calamari, rinsed and roughly sliced into 1 cm rings or slices

1 Tbsp lemon juice

handful roughly chopped fresh basil or parsley

salt and freshly ground black pepper

CIABATTA TOASTS

2 ciabatta rolls

1 clove garlic

olive oil, for drizzling

Parmesan shavings

WHAT TO DO

1. Heat the olive oil in a frying pan and fry the garlic and chilli for 2 minutes, or until the garlic has softened but not coloured.

2. Add the canned tomatoes, thyme, sugar and stock, and leave to simmer on medium heat for 15 minutes.

3. Add the fish fillets, put the lid on, and leave to poach for about 4 minutes, or until they are almost cooked through. Add the mussels and calamari and poach for another 3–4 minutes, or until the mussels have opened. Remove from the heat, discard any mussels that have not opened, stir through the lemon juice and fresh basil or parsley and add a generous pinch of salt and freshly ground black pepper.

4. In the meantime, preheat the oven's grill to the highest setting, slice the ciabatta rolls in half (or four to six slices), and place under the grill for 2–3 minutes until golden. Remove, rub gently two or three times on each side with the garlic clove, drizzle with olive oil and top with Parmesan shavings.

5. Spoon the seafood in its sauce into warm soup bowls, and serve with the ciabatta toasts on the side. Alternatively, serve over angel-hair pasta.

snacks.

SPEEDY SMOKED SNOEK PÂTÉ.

I LOVE THE SOUTH-AFRICANNESS OF SMOKED SNOEK, AND I LOVE TO MAKE IT JUST A LITTLE POSH BY MIXING IT INTO THIS CREAMY HERBED PÂTÉ AND SPREADING IT OVER CRUNCHY BRUSCHETTA OR STILL-WARM BAGUETTE. PERFECT PICNIC FOOD FOR ALFRESCO FEASTING.

SERVES 4 | PREPARATION TIME 10–15 minutes

WHAT YOU'LL NEED

200 g smoked snoek (not previously frozen)
200 g plain cottage cheese (smooth or chunky)
100 ml double-thick yoghurt
1 Tbsp each chopped fresh basil and parsley
1 Tbsp lemon juice
1 tsp lemon zest
salt and freshly ground black pepper to taste
fresh crusty bread, for serving

WHAT TO DO

1. Using your hands, flake the snoek into small pieces in a medium-sized mixing bowl, and be sure to remove any bones. If necessary, use a knife to chop the meat smaller for a smoother end result.
2. Add the remaining ingredients and mix well. Check for seasoning and serve immediately with fresh crusty bread, or refrigerate in a sealed container for 2–3 days.

Note: You could easily use mackerel, trout or salmon instead of snoek.

SWEETCORN POT BREAD
with Blistered Tomatoes.

IF YOU MAKE THIS, EAT ONE SLICE AND VERY QUICKLY GIVE THE REST AWAY, BECAUSE IT'S COMPLETELY AND UT-TERLY IRRESISTIBLE. FROM THE MOMENT THE CREAMY, CHEESY, CORN-FILLED AROMA STARTS TO SNEAK OUT OF THE OVEN YOU'LL BE FIGHTING A LOSING BATTLE. AND IF YOU'RE A HAPPY LOSER, WELL THEN ADD LOTS OF THICK, COLD BUTTER. AND IF YOU CAN'T BE BOTHERED TO MAKE THE TOMATO JAM, JUST USE A JAR OF ONION MARMALADE OR APRICOT JAM. HEAVEN.

SERVES 4–6 | PREPARATION TIME 10 minutes | COOKING TIME 40–50 minutes (mostly unattended)

WHAT YOU'LL NEED

SWEETCORN POT BREAD

3 eggs

500 g self-raising flour

350 ml buttermilk or natural yoghurt
   (or 1 x 340 ml can beer)

1 cup grated Cheddar cheese (you could
   also add in some crumbled feta)

1 small onion, grated or very finely
   chopped

2–3 sprigs fresh thyme

generous pinch each of salt and freshly
   ground black pepper

1 x 410 g can whole kernel corn

BLISTERED TOMATOES

1 cup rosa or cherry tomatoes, halved

1–2 sprigs fresh thyme

1–2 tsp sugar

1 Tbsp balsamic vinegar

generous pinch each of salt and freshly
   ground black pepper

WHAT TO DO

1. Preheat the oven to 180 °C and line a loaf tin with baking paper (or use the pot and fire method, see notes below).
2. Mix all the bread ingredients together, spoon into the loaf tin and bake for 40–45 minutes, or until the loaf is golden and when a sharp knife inserted in the centre comes out clean.
3. Meanwhile, add all of the ingredients for the blistered tomatoes to a small saucepan and cook for 12–15 minutes on medium-low heat until sticky. Add a little water to the pot if necessary. Remove from the heat, check for seasoning and set aside.
4. Serve the bread within a few minutes of removing from the oven, with lashings of fresh butter and the blistered tomatoes on the side.

Notes: The dough can also be shaped into individual bread rolls.
Campfire method: Place the bread dough into a lightly greased cast-iron pot, cover with the lid and place over hot coals. Also place a few coals on top of the lid. Change the coals from time to time with new hot ones and leave to cook for about 40 minutes.
To make quick buttermilk, add 1 Tbsp lemon juice to 2 cups full-cream milk and leave to stand for 15 minutes. The mixture will curdle into buttermilk.

PITA BREADS.

OH HOW I LOVE A FLATBREAD. THEY ARE SO VERSATILE AND WELL-LOVED THAT THEY EVEN HAVE COUSINS IN ALL CORNERS OR THE WORLD – PITA BREADS; ROTIS; NAAN'S – ALL SIMPLE, BEAUTIFUL BLANK CANVASSES FOR SO MANY AMAZING FLAVOURS AND FILLINGS. AND BELIEVE ME WHEN I SAY THAT THEY REALLY DO TASTE DOUBLY AMAZING WHEN YOU MAKE THEM FROM SCRATCH.

PREPARATION TIME 10 minutes | COOKING TIME 10 minutes

WHAT YOU'LL NEED

1 cup self-raising flour
½ cup double-thick natural yoghurt
½ tsp finely chopped fresh rosemary
½ tsp salt
pinch of freshly ground black pepper

WHAT TO DO

1. Mix all the ingredients together in a large mixing bowl in the stand of your electric mixer with the dough hook attachment. Add extra flour if necessary, but the dough should be quite wet and sticky. When the dough comes together, knead for 2–3 minutes on a lightly floured surface.
2. Take a golf ball-sized piece of dough and roll out as thinly as possible with a floured rolling pin, again on a floured surface.
3. Fry the pitas, one at a time, in a dry frying pan over high heat. Allow each side to blister and turn golden brown before removing from the pan. Wipe the pan down with kitchen paper, and repeat until you have used all the dough.

ROSEMARY *STOKBROOD.*

STOKBROOD TRANSLATES SIMPLY TO 'STICK BREAD' FROM AFRIKAANS. IT'S PERFECTION. SOFT DOUGH ROASTED ON THE END OF A STICK OVER HOT COALS MEANS THAT IT'S SMOKY AND BLISTERED BUT NOT BURNT; CRUSTY ON THE OUTSIDE AND SOFT AND FLUFFY ON THE INSIDE. TEAR IT OPEN AND FILL WITH SLIVERS OF HARD CHEESE AND APRICOT JAM (OR THE BACON AND CLEMENTINE MARMALADE ON PAGE 15) FOR A CAMPFIRE SNACK, OR SAVE IT FOR DUNKING IN SLOW-COOKED ANYTHING.

MAKES about 10 rolls | PREPARATION TIME 1 hour (mostly unattended) | COOKING TIME 15–20 minutes (plus resting and rising time)

WHAT YOU'LL NEED

500 g cake flour
1 tsp salt
1 Tbsp sugar
1 tsp dried rosemary
2 Tbsp olive oil or melted butter
1 x 10 g sachet instant yeast
250–300 ml lukewarm water (or 200 ml water and 100 ml milk or buttermilk)
clean arm-length sticks, soaked in water, for cooking

WHAT TO DO

1. Mix all the ingredients, except the water, together. Slowly add the water until the mixture comes together in a soft dough. This can be done by hand or in a food processor or stand mixer with dough hook attached.
2. Knead the dough on a lightly floured surface for 5–10 minutes, or until it is smooth and elastic. Place in a lightly oiled bowl and cover with a damp cloth or clingfilm. Leave to rest and rise for 30 minutes.
3. Divide into equal palm-sized portions and roll each portion until it is about 20 cm long, then wind it around the stick and gently press it all together. Cook over medium-hot coals until golden and just cooked through, 10–15 minutes.

BAKED CAMEMBERT IN PHYLLO
with Quick Thyme and Fig Jam.

OH, THE DECADENCE! THERE'S GORGEOUSLY GLOSSY MELTED CHEESE AND THE DELICATE SNAP OF GOLDEN PHYLLO PASTRY, AND THEN THERE'S THE STICKY SWEETNESS OF THE ROASTED FIGS.

SERVES 4 | PREPARATION TIME 10–15 minutes | COOKING TIME 20–25 minutes

WHAT YOU'LL NEED

1 Tbsp butter

2 tsp soft brown sugar

2 tsp balsamic vinegar

1 sprig fresh thyme

3 ripe figs, roughly chopped (or canned, juice drained)

1–2 Tbsp water or orange juice

4 sheets phyllo pastry

3–4 Tbsp melted butter

1 round Camembert (or Brie) cheese

WHAT TO DO

1. Preheat the oven to 180 °C and grease a baking tray.
2. Add the butter to a medium-sized saucepan over medium heat and when it starts to foam add the sugar, balsamic vinegar, thyme and figs. Simmer gently for about 10 minutes, or until the figs have softened and start to become sticky. Turn down the heat if the figs start to burn, and add the water or orange juice for extra liquid, if required.
3. Meanwhile, on a clean work surface, lay out one sheet of phyllo pastry at a time and brush with melted butter. Keep the remaining sheets covered with a damp, clean dishcloth as you work; this prevents them from drying out. Once you have brushed one sheet, lay the next sheet over the buttered one, brush with melted butter, and repeat until you have used all four sheets. Turn the stack of sheets over and brush the underside with melted butter too.
4. Place the cheese in the centre of the pastry sheets, spoon over the thyme and fig jam, gather the corners together and twist at the top. Secure with kitchen string if necessary. Gently place the pastry package onto the baking tray and place in the oven for 20–25 minutes, or until the pastry is golden.
5. Remove from the oven and serve warm with fresh farm bread or crunchy crostini.

SALT AND PEPPER SQUID
with Basil and Lemon Mayonnaise.

CRISPY, CRUNCHY, GOLDEN FLASH-FRIED SQUID IS ALWAYS EASY TO LOVE. HERE, WITH THE CREAMY BASIL AND LEMON MAYONNAISE, IT REALLY SINGS.

SERVES 4–6 | PREPARATION TIME 10 minutes | COOKING TIME 5 minutes

WHAT YOU'LL NEED

vegetable oil, for frying
$1/2$ cup cake flour
$1/4$ cup cornflour
1 tsp sea salt flakes
$1/2$ tsp freshly ground black pepper
$1/2$ tsp dried chilli flakes (optional)
500 g fresh calamari, cut into 5 mm rings, rinsed and patted dry with kitchen paper or a clean dishcloth

BASIL AND LEMON MAYONNAISE

1 egg
1 clove garlic
$1/2$ avocado, de-pipped, peeled and roughly chopped
2 Tbsp lemon juice
1–2 Tbsp chopped fresh basil
pinch each of salt and freshly ground black pepper
$3/4$ cup cooking oil (not olive oil)

WHAT TO DO

1. Pour the vegetable oil into a wok or large saucepan until it is about 1 cm deep and place over a medium-high heat.
2. Meanwhile, combine the flour, cornflour, salt, pepper and chilli flakes (if using). Put the calamari rings in a large sieve set over a mixing bowl, pour over the flour and spice mixture and toss gently to coat.
3. After a minute or two, check that the oil is hot enough by dropping in a calamari ring. It should be golden and crispy in 1 minute.
4. Drop the calamari rings into the oil, one at a time, and fry for 3–5 minutes or until lightly golden. Remove using a slotted spoon and set aside to drain on two layers of kitchen paper.
5. Make the mayonnaise as follows: To a blender, add all the ingredients, except the oil. Then slowly drizzle in the oil in a constant stream with the blender on a low speed. Continue blending until all the oil is incorporated and the mixture thickens to the usual consistency of mayonnaise.
6. Serve the calamari immediately with the basil and lemon mayonnaise as a dipping sauce.

Notes: For a speedier version of the Basil and Lemon Mayonnaise, use 1 cup good-quality mayonnaise mixed with the lemon juice, basil, salt and pepper.
The Basil and Lemon Mayonnaise makes about 1 cup, so there will be leftovers. Store in an airtight container in the fridge for up to four days. If not using avocado for the mayonnaise, use 1 cup of oil.

BBQ CHICKEN WINGS
with Creamy Whipped Feta.

WHAT COULD POSSIBLY GO WRONG WHEN STICKY, GLOSSY, GOLDEN CHICKEN WINGS MEET CREAMY, SALTY WHIPPED FETA? THIS IS ONE OF MY FAVOURITE SNACKS AND I HOPE YOU'LL GIVE IT A BASH.

SERVES 4 | PREPARATION TIME 10 minutes | COOKING TIME 20 minutes

WHAT YOU'LL NEED
8–10 chicken wings

BBQ SAUCE
2 Tbsp olive oil
2 Tbsp tomato ketchup
1 Tbsp balsamic vinegar
2 Tbsp runny honey
2 Tbsp light brown sugar
1 Tbsp lemon juice
1 tsp paprika
½ tsp dried coriander
2 cloves garlic, minced
generous pinch each of salt and freshly
   ground black pepper

CREAMY WHIPPED FETA
75 g feta cheese
100 g smooth plain cottage cheese
zest of 1 lemon
1 Tbsp lemon juice
2 Tbsp olive oil or milk, to loosen if
   necessary
1 Tbsp chopped fresh basil or mint
freshly ground black pepper and olive oil,
   for garnishing

WHAT TO DO
1. Combine all the sauce ingredients in a jug or mixing bowl.
2. Baste the chicken with the sauce, cover with clingfilm and leave to stand in the fridge for as long as possible before cooking (overnight is ideal, but not essential). Remove from the fridge and bring to room temperature about 20 minutes before cooking.
3. Cook on the braai, or roast in the oven at 180 °C, for 20–25 minutes or until cooked through, sticky and golden. Baste with any extra sauce every 10 minutes or so during cooking.
4. Combine all the ingredients for the whipped feta in a food processor and mix until well combined. Check for seasoning and spoon into a serving bowl. Garnish with a drizzle of olive oil and a twist of black pepper.
5. As soon as the wings are cooked, serve immediately with the whipped feta on the side.

Notes: Leave out the sugar in the BBQ sauce for a healthier but less sticky option.
Use thick natural yoghurt instead of cottage cheese for the Creamy Whipped Feta.

STICKY ASIAN RIBS.

I DARE YOU TO TELL ME THAT YOU ARE ABLE TO RESIST THE WILES OF STICKY, GOLDEN, FINGER-LICKING RIBS. WITH THE SPICY ASIAN-INSPIRED SAUCE THEY HAVE A LITTLE EXTRA *JE NE SAIS QUOI*, AND I THINK IT'S PRETTY AMAZING.

SERVES 4–6 | PREPARATION TIME 15 minutes | COOKING TIME 30–40 minutes (mostly unattended)

WHAT YOU'LL NEED

⅓ **cup runny honey**

⅓ **cup soy sauce**

2 Tbsp olive oil

2 Tbsp fish sauce

2 Tbsp oyster sauce

⅓ **cup water**

½ **tsp Chinese five-spice**

2 tsp grated fresh ginger

2 cloves garlic, minced

½ **tsp dried chilli flakes**

1 kg pork ribs, cut into individual riblets

1–2 Tbsp toasted sesame seeds (optional), for serving

1 Tbsp chopped fresh coriander, for serving

WHAT TO DO

1. Preheat the oven to 200 °C.
2. Prepare the marinade by adding the honey, soy sauce, olive oil, fish sauce, oyster sauce, water, five-spice, ginger, garlic and chilli to a shallow baking dish lined with tinfoil (for easy cleaning later). Mix the marinade until well combined. Then add the riblets and toss until they are well coated.
3. Place in the oven for 40 minutes, or until sticky and golden and the meat is cooked through, tossing every 10–15 minutes.
4. Serve immediately as a snack with a sprinkling of sesame seeds (if using) and fresh coriander. You can also add a nice leafy green side salad and potato wedges for a main meal.

HONEY AND SESAME PRAWN STICKS.

WE'VE WILED AWAY MANY HAPPY MOMENTS ON MOZAMBICAN BEACHES, WHERE YOU CAN BUY FRESH SEAFOOD FROM THE FISHERMEN RIGHT OUT OF THE WATER. THESE ARE ONE OF MY FAVOURITE THINGS TO FEAST ON AS THE SUN GOES DOWN ON ANOTHER GORGEOUS DAY.

SERVES 4 | PREPARATION TIME 15 minutes (plus 30 minutes marinating time, optional)
COOKING TIME approx. 6 minutes

WHAT YOU'LL NEED
8 bamboo skewers
400 g whole prawns, deveined (shells optional)
1 clove garlic, crushed
1 tsp freshly grated ginger
3 Tbsp honey
1 Tbsp sesame oil
2 Tbsp soy sauce
1 Tbsp chopped fresh coriander, basil or mint
lime wedges, for serving

WHAT TO DO
1. Soak the bamboo skewers in water for about 15 minutes to prevent them catching fire when cooking.
2. Rinse the prawns and set them aside to dry. If using immediately, pat dry with kitchen paper. Skewer about three prawns onto each stick, heads and tails almost touching to make a 'u' shape, or use two skewers as shown. Set aside in a wide, shallow dish.
3. Mix the remaining ingredients, except the fresh herbs and lime wedges, and pour half of the sauce over the prawns, making sure each is well coated. Leave to marinate for 30 minutes if you have the time.
4. Cook over hot coals or a preheated griddle pan for 3 minutes on each side, or until pink and just cooked through. Serve immediately with a sprinkling of fresh herbs and lime wedges, and the extra sauce on the side.

RICOTTA BRUSCHETTA
with Courgettes and Mint.

I LOVE TURNING SIMPLE, HUMBLE INGREDIENTS INTO SOMETHING SPECIAL. 'JUST' COURGETTES ARE FLASH-FRIED UNTIL GOLDEN AND THEN PERCHED PROUDLY ATOP CRUNCHY BRUSCHETTA ALONG WITH CREAMY RICOTTA AND LASHINGS OF FRESH MINT. IT'S HEAVEN TO EAT.

SERVES 6–8 | PREPARATION TIME 5–10 minutes | COOKING TIME 10 minutes

---

WHAT YOU'LL NEED

1 day-old baguette, cut diagonally into
   1-cm-thick slices
200 g courgettes, sliced into ribbons with
   a vegetable peeler
salt and freshly ground black pepper
1 Tbsp olive oil
100 g ricotta
100 ml natural yoghurt
1 tsp chopped fresh mint, plus extra whole
   leaves for serving
zest of 1 lemon
extra 1–2 tsp olive oil
lemon juice (optional)

WHAT TO DO

1. Preheat the oven on the grill setting. Lay the baguette slices flat on a baking tray. Grill for 2–3 minutes on each side or until lightly golden.
2. Season and fry the courgette ribbons in the olive oil over medium-high heat until lightly golden. Remove and drain on kitchen paper.
3. Meanwhile, roughly mix together the ricotta, yoghurt, mint, lemon zest and olive oil. Season with salt and pepper.
4. To assemble, spread each bruschetta slice with some of the ricotta and herb mix, top with a few courgette ribbons and a few loose mint leaves, add an extra drizzle of olive oil and some lemon juice (if you like), and serve immediately.

COURGETTE AND MINT RÖSTIS
with Cucumber Raita.

WHAT COULD POSSIBLY GO WRONG WHEN YOU ADD BEAUTIFULLY FLUFFY AND GOLDEN LITTLE MINTED COURGETTE RÖSTIS, WHICH ARE LIKE SMALL PANCAKES, TO A FRESH CUCUMBER YOGHURT DIP?

MAKES 6 | PREPARATION TIME 10 minutes | COOKING TIME 10–15 minutes

WHAT YOU'LL NEED
CUCUMBER RAITA
200 ml natural yoghurt
½ cucumber, deseeded and finely diced
1 Tbsp finely chopped fresh mint leaves
zest of ½ lemon
½ tsp salt
pinch of freshly ground black pepper

RÖSTIS
250 g courgettes (about 8 medium-sized ones), grated and any excess moisture squeezed out
½ cup frozen baby peas
100 g feta cheese, crumbled
1 egg, lightly beaten
2 Tbsp cake flour
1 Tbsp chopped fresh mint
salt and freshly ground black pepper
6 Tbsp cooking oil

WHAT TO DO
1. For the raita, combine all the ingredients and chill until ready to serve.
2. Combine all the rösti ingredients, except the oil, in a mixing bowl, and then set aside. (Note: I used the grater function on my food processor to grate the courgettes, super quick, and then I squeezed out extra moisture using kitchen paper.)
3. Heat half the oil in a heavy-bottomed pan on medium-high heat. After a couple of minutes, test to check that the oil is hot enough by dropping in a drop of the batter. If it bubbles and turns golden brown within 15 seconds, it is ready.
4. Add 1 heaped Tbsp of the rösti mixture to the pan. Flatten with the back of a spoon and repeat until you have three röstis in the pan. Cook for about 3 minutes on each side, or until golden brown. Remove and set aside on a plate lined with kitchen paper. Repeat with the remaining oil and rösti mixture.
5. Eat the röstis as soon as they are cooked, and serve with dollops of fresh raita on the side.

SATAY PRAWN STICKS.

PERFECTLY PINK, PLUMP PRAWNS MEET A SILKY SMOOTH PEANUTTY SAUCE AND, WELL, FIREWORKS.

SERVES 4 | PREPARATION TIME 5–10 minutes | COOKING TIME 15–20 minutes

WHAT YOU'LL NEED

SATAY SAUCE
1 Tbsp chopped fresh coriander
1 fresh chilli, deseeded and finely chopped
1 clove garlic, crushed
2 Tbsp peanut butter
1 Tbsp soy sauce
1 tsp grated fresh ginger
¼ cup coconut milk
zest and juice of 1 lime
1–2 Tbsp honey

PRAWNS
36–40 prawns, deveined and shelled
bamboo skewers
1 Tbsp olive oil
fresh coriander leaves, for serving
lime or lemon juice, for serving

WHAT TO DO

1. Mix the satay sauce ingredients together until smooth.
2. Thread about three prawns onto each bamboo skewer, with their nose and tail touching so that they make a 'u' shape. Trim each skewer so that it is 6–8 cm long. Lay the skewers in a shallow baking dish and pour over three-quarters of the sauce, along with a drizzle of olive oil, and toss to make sure they are well coated.
3. Fry in a hot pan for 5 minutes or until pink and cooked through, turning halfway. Drizzle over the remaining sauce and serve immediately with an extra squeeze of lime or lemon juice, and a scattering of fresh coriander leaves.

PEAR AND GORGONZOLA TARTLETS.

THIS COMBINATION OF GOLDEN, FLAKY PASTRY TOPPED PROUDLY WITH ROASTED PEARS AND MELTED GORGONZOLA IS ALWAYS A CROWD PLEASER. AND AS WITH SO MANY CLEVER QUICK-FIXES, THE VARIATIONS ARE ENDLESS. TRY ROASTED BEETROOT AND CRUMBLE OVER GOAT'S CHEESE JUST BEFORE SERVING, OR BUTTERNUT CUBES WITH PINE NUTS AND FETA.

SERVES 6–8 | PREPARATION TIME 15 minutes | COOKING TIME 15 minutes

WHAT YOU'LL NEED

1 sheet ready-made puff pastry, thawed

4 Tbsp chutney or onion marmalade

3 ripe pears, skin on, halved and sliced lengthways

1–2 Tbsp melted butter or olive oil

100 g Gorgonzola cheese (or Brie for a milder taste)

balsamic reduction, for serving (optional)

handful fresh rocket, for garnishing

WHAT TO DO

1. Preheat the oven to 180 °C and lightly grease a baking tray.
2. Roll out the puff pastry on a lightly floured surface and cut into 8–10 equal squares. Place the squares on the baking tray.
3. Prick each square with a fork two or three times, then spread a thin layer of chutney or onion marmalade over each one, leaving a small border around the edges. Top with a few pear slices brushed with melted butter or olive oil, and add some roughly crumbled cheese.
4. Bake for 20–25 minutes, or until the pastry is golden and the cheese has melted.
5. Remove from the oven and allow to cool for a few minutes. Transfer to a serving platter, drizzle with a little balsamic reduction (if using), scatter over the fresh rocket and serve immediately.

meat.

CIDER AND CLEMENTINE PORK BELLY
with Roasted Carrot Mash.

A SLOW-COOKED PORK BELLY HAS TO BE ONE OF MY FAVOURITE THINGS. IT ALWAYS CATCHES MY EYE ON RESTAURANT MENUS AND WINS MY HEART EVERY TIME. HERE, WITH THE SYRUPY CIDER AND CLEMENTINE SAUCE, IT REALLY STANDS TALL.

SERVES 4–6 | PREPARATION TIME 10 minutes | COOKING TIME approx. 3½ hours (mostly unattended)

WHAT YOU'LL NEED

- 1–2 tsp sea salt flakes
- 1–2 Tbsp olive oil
- 1.5 kg pork belly, scored (or use boneless pork loin)
- 1 x 340 ml can cider
- juice of 1 clementine or orange
- 1 thumb-sized stick of fresh ginger, roughly chopped
- 2 Tbsp light brown sugar or chutney
- 4 large carrots, roughly chopped
- ½ tsp ground coriander
- knob of butter, for serving
- salt and freshly ground black pepper

WHAT TO DO

1. Preheat the oven to 220 °C and line a deep baking tray with tinfoil (for easier cleaning later).
2. Rub about 1 tsp sea salt flakes and a drizzle of olive oil into the skin of the pork belly and into the scoring marks.
3. Place the pork in the baking tray and add the remaining ingredients, ending with a sprinkling of ground coriander over the carrots. Roast for 30 minutes on the middle shelf at 220 °C, then turn the heat down to 170 °C and roast for a further 2½–3 hours, or until the crackling is crisp and the meat is cooked through. Leave to rest for 15–20 minutes before carving and serving.
4. While the meat rests, remove the carrots from the roasting tray and mash roughly with a knob of butter. Add salt and pepper to taste.
5. Serve the pork with the carrot mash and a drizzle of the pan juices.

Note: Add a bowl of steaming olive-oil dressed peas on the side to add some extra colour.

STICKY GINGER AND HOISIN PORK
with Pak choi and Noodles.

THIS IS STIR-FRYING AT ITS BEST. SUPER SPEEDY AND FULL OF PUNCHY ASIAN FLAVOURS, AND WHEN YOU BRING IT ALL TOGETHER WITH ITS DARK AND GLOSSY SAUCE, IT'S HONEST TO GOODNESSLY DELICIOUS.

SERVES 4 | PREPARATION TIME 15 minutes | COOKING TIME 15 minutes

WHAT YOU'LL NEED

1 Tbsp cooking oil

750 g pork fillet, cut into 2 cm cubes
 or strips

1 heaped tsp grated fresh ginger

2 spring onions, sliced diagonally, including
 the tops

1 fresh chilli, deseeded and finely sliced

1 clove garlic, chopped

3 Tbsp hoisin sauce

1 Tbsp soy sauce

1 Tbsp sesame oil

1 Tbsp honey

4–6 heads baby pak choi, halved lengthways (or Savoy cabbage or baby spinach)

400 g udon or rice noodles

lime wedges, for serving

1–2 Tbsp chopped fresh coriander or basil,
 for serving

2 Tbsp salted peanuts or slivered almonds,
 for serving

WHAT TO DO

1. Heat the cooking oil in a heavy-based pan over medium-high heat and add the pork along with the ginger, spring onions and chilli. Fry for 3–4 minutes, or until the pork is starting to caramelise on the outside.
2. Lower the heat to medium-low and add the garlic, hoisin sauce, soy sauce, sesame oil and honey and cook for another minute. Add the pak choi, cabbage or spinach and toss gently, then leave to cook for another 1–2 minutes, or until the pak choi has wilted.
3. Meanwhile, prepare the udon or rice noodles according to the packet instructions.
4. To serve, divide the noodles between warmed bowls and spoon over the pork and pak choi. Add a drizzle of the sauce from the pan, a generous squeeze of lime juice, sprinkle over the chopped herbs and nuts, and serve immediately.

Note: This recipe would also work well served with ½ cup jasmine rice, cooked according to packet instructions.

WORS ROLLS
with Pear and Red Onion Relish.

OH HOW WE LOVE A BOERIE ROLL IN SOUTH AFRICA. THEY ARE, UNASHAMEDLY, ONE OF MY VERY FAVOURITE THINGS TO EAT. IT'S REALLY JUST A SIMPLE SAUSAGE, USUALLY MADE FROM BEEF OR LAMB, AND IT'S COOKED LOVINGLY OVER BLISTERING HOT COALS AND SERVED IN A STILL-WARM BREAD ROLL. WHEN YOU ADD THE PEAR AND ONION RELISH, THIS BECOMES A CLASSIC CASE OF SOMETHING BEING SO MUCH MORE THAN THE SUM OF ITS SIMPLE PARTS.

SERVES 4 | PREPARATION TIME 15 minutes | COOKING TIME approx. 20 minutes

WHAT YOU'LL NEED

PEAR AND ONION RELISH

1 Tbsp olive oil

1 Tbsp butter

1 large or 2 medium-sized red onions, chopped

2 tsp lemon juice

1 sprig fresh rosemary

4 ripe pears, peeled, cored and roughly chopped

2–3 tsp light brown sugar

pinch each of salt and freshly ground black pepper

WORS ROLLS

4–6 pieces of good-quality beef or lamb boerewors

salt and freshly ground black pepper

4–6 fresh hotdog rolls, sliced in half and lightly buttered

WHAT TO DO

1. For the relish, heat the olive oil and butter in a heavy-based frying pan over medium-high heat. Add the onion and cook for 7–10 minutes, or until they have softened. Add the remaining ingredients, turn down the heat and leave to simmer for about 10 minutes, or until the pears can be roughly mashed with a fork. Check for seasoning and set aside.

2. Meanwhile, for the wors rolls, season the boerewors lightly with salt and pepper and cook over a braai or in a griddle pan over medium-high heat for 15–20 minutes, or until the meat is just cooked through.

3. Place a piece of wors into each roll and top with a generous spoonful of pear and onion relish. Serve immediately.

Note: This relish works just as well with apples, and you can also cut the rolls in half and serve them as snacks.

SIRLOIN STEAK SARMIES
with Chimichurri and Roasted Tomatoes.

A STEAK SARMIE CAN SO EASILY BE JUST A STEAK SARMIE. HERE, WITH THE SEARED SIRLOIN AND ZESTY, FRESH, HERBY CHIMICHURRI (SOUTH AMERICA'S ANSWER TO PESTO OR GREMOLATA), IT CAN SIT PROUDLY AT ANY TABLE. I'VE MADE THESE INTO OPEN SANDWICHES SO THAT YOU USE JUST ONE SLICE OF BREAD, BUT YOU CAN ALSO TURN THIS INTO A CARB-FREE FEAST AND SERVE THE STEAK OVER A SIMPLE SALAD.

SERVES 4 | PREPARATION TIME 10 minutes | COOKING TIME 10–15 minutes

WHAT YOU'LL NEED
1 Tbsp olive oil, plus extra for drizzling
400–500 g sirloin steak, lightly seasoned
    with salt and freshly ground black
    pepper
1 Tbsp butter
2 whole cloves garlic
1 cup rosa or cherry tomatoes
4 slices ciabatta or sourdough bread
1 small red onion, thinly sliced
small handful roughly torn fresh flat-leaf
    parsley, for serving

CHIMICHURRI
2 Tbsp chopped fresh flat-leaf parsley
1 Tbsp chopped fresh coriander or oregano
1 clove garlic , crushed
$\frac{1}{2}$–1 fresh chilli, deseeded and chopped
$\frac{1}{2}$ tsp salt
2 Tbsp lemon juice (or red wine vinegar)
2 Tbsp olive oil

WHAT TO DO
1. Add the olive oil to a large pan over medium-high heat. Add the steaks and cook for 3–4 minutes (depending on thickness), then turn over and add the butter and garlic cloves (you don't want to add the butter at the start as it might burn). Cook for a further 3–4 minutes and then remove the steak from the pan and set aside to rest.
2. Fry the tomatoes in the same pan as you used for the steak, for 3–4 minutes, or until they have softened and are starting to colour. Mash roughly with a fork, season with a little salt and pepper and set aside.
3. Make the chimichurri by blitzing all the ingredients together using a stick blender or pestle and mortar.
4. Slice the steak diagonally into thin slivers. Drizzle the bread with a little olive oil and toast in a dry pan or under the grill until golden.
5. To assemble, spoon some tomatoes over each slice of bread, followed by a few slices of red onion. Top with the steak and a generous drizzle of chimichurri. Garnish with a few extra parsley leaves and serve immediately.

SPRINGBOK FILLET
with Roasted Beetroot and Mozzarella Salad with Watercress Dressing.

I GREW UP EATING VENISON AND AM RIGHT AT HOME WITH IT. IT'S WONDERFULLY LEAN, HEALTHY AND VERSATILE. SOME PEOPLE JUST CAN'T DO IT THOUGH, SO IF YOU'RE ONE OF THOSE THEN YOU ARE WELCOME TO MAKE THIS USING BEEF FILLET, OR EVEN SIMPLE LAMB CHOPS.

SERVES 4–6 | PREPARATION TIME 10 minutes | COOKING TIME 30 minutes

WHAT YOU'LL NEED

SPRINGBOK
1 kg springbok fillet or deboned leg
1 Tbsp butter
2 Tbsp olive oil
1 clove garlic, mashed
1 heaped tsp Dijon mustard
zest of 1 lemon
juice of ½ lemon
1 Tbsp brandy
generous pinch of salt and freshly ground
    black pepper

BEETROOT AND MOZZARELLA SALAD
4–6 fresh beetroot
salt and freshly ground black pepper
handful mixed salad leaves
100 g mozzarella cheese
small handful toasted pine nuts, or any
    roughly chopped roasted nuts, for serving

WATERCRESS DRESSING
40 g watercress
zest and juice of 1 lemon
2–3 Tbsp olive oil
pinch each of salt and sugar

WHAT TO DO

1. Remove the fillet from the fridge about an hour before you start cooking so that it can reach room temperature. About 10 minutes before you start cooking, preheat the oven to 180 °C.
2. Remove the stems from the beetroot (using kitchen gloves if necessary to avoid staining your hands). Simmer the beetroot in a saucepan, with enough water to cover them, over medium-high heat for about 40 minutes, or until cooked through and they can be easily pierced with a knife. Drain and set aside to cool.
3. When cooled, peel and quarter the beetroot. Season with salt and pepper and set aside.
4. Mix the remaining springbok ingredients together to make a basting and coat the fillet with the mixture.
5. Sear the fillet with 1 Tbsp extra olive oil in a heavy-based pan over medium-high heat, turning until all sides are golden. Then transfer to the oven and roast for a further 10 minutes. Remove from the heat, cover with tinfoil and leave to rest for at least 10 minutes.
6. Just before serving, mix all the dressing ingredients together in a pestle and mortar until you have a loose dressing. Place the salad leaves on a platter and add the beetroot and roughly torn pieces of mozzarella. Drizzle over the dressing and scatter over the pine nuts.
7. Thinly slice the fillet and arrange on a warmed serving platter. Serve with the salad.

Note: Use butternut or sweet potato instead of beetroot, and feta or goat's cheese instead of mozzarella in the salad.

BEER AND BRISKET PIE
with Rough Puff Pastry.

THIS IS ABOUT AS MANLY AS A MEAL CAN GET, BUT DON'T LET THAT PUT YOU OFF, IT'S ENDLESSLY EASY TO EAT. YOU CAN USE READY-MADE PUFF PASTRY FOR THE LID IF YOU DON'T HAVE TIME TO MAKE THE VERSION SHOWN HERE.

SERVES 4 | PREPARATION TIME 10 minutes | COOKING TIME approx. 1½ hours (mostly unattended)

WHAT YOU'LL NEED

2 Tbsp olive oil

1 kg diced beef brisket, without bones
   (or any other stewing steak)

2 Tbsp cake flour, seasoned with salt and
   freshly ground black pepper

3–4 sprigs fresh thyme or 1 tsp dried

1 sprig fresh rosemary or 1 tsp dried

1 medium-sized red onion, chopped

1 large clove garlic, finely chopped

1 Tbsp Worcestershire sauce

2 Tbsp tomato ketchup

1 Tbsp Dijon mustard

1 x 340 ml bottle beer

1 cup beef or vegetable stock

1 large sweet potato, peeled and chopped

1 cup roughly chopped carrots

salt and freshly ground black pepper

1 cup water

ROUGH PUFF PASTRY

250 g cake flour

1 tsp salt

200 g cold butter

about 150 ml cold water or milk

1 tsp lemon juice or white wine vinegar

WHAT TO DO

1. Heat the olive oil in a medium-sized ovenproof pan or skillet over medium-high heat. Toss the beef in the seasoned flour, dusting off any excess, and fry for 3–4 minutes until golden on both sides. Remove with a slotted spoon and set aside.

2. Add the thyme, rosemary and onion to the same pan and leave to cook on medium-low heat for 10 minutes, or until the onion has softened. Add the garlic and cook for another minute. Return the beef to the pan, along with the Worcestershire sauce, tomato ketchup, mustard, beer and stock, and simmer for 45 minutes, or until the meat is tender.

3. Add the sweet potato and carrots, ensuring they are covered with liquid. Season to taste. Add the water as needed.

4. Leave to simmer with the lid off for a further 15–20 minutes, or until the sweet potato is soft, the meat is tender and the sauce starts to thicken. Add a little more stock or water if you find the mixture is getting too dry.

5. Meanwhile, make the rough puff pastry (or alternatively use ready-made puff pastry). Sift the flour and salt into a large bowl. Roughly cut the butter into small cubes, add them to the bowl and mix them in loosely using a metal spoon or palette knife, 'cutting the butter into the flour' until all the pieces of butter are well coated in flour and the mixture has a crumbly consistency.

6. Gently pour in about two-thirds of the cold water or milk and the lemon juice or vinegar, mixing until you have a rough dough, adding extra water if needed. Try to avoid hard kneading of the dough.

7. Turn the dough out onto a lightly floured surface and shape into a smooth, rectangular slab. Roll the dough in one direction, away from yourself, until it is about three times the original length, about 15 x 30 cm. If needed, sprinkle over a little extra flour while rolling. Keep the edges neat and even. Don't overwork the butter; you are aiming for a marbled effect.

8. Fold the top third of the pastry down to the centre, then fold the bottom third up and over that. Give the dough a quarter turn (to the left or right) and roll out again to three times the length. Repeat twice more and fold as before, then wrap with clingfilm and refrigerate for at least 30 minutes before allowing to warm almost to room temperature and then rolling to use. Roll out to 5–7 mm thick.

9. Preheat the oven to 180 °C. Place the beef stew in a suitable lightly greased baking dish (you want the filling to be almost level with the top of the dish). Cover the beef filling with the pastry, brush with a lightly beaten egg and prick the pastry a few times with a fork to allow the steam to escape while baking. Bake in the middle of the oven for 15–20 minutes, or until the pastry is crisp and golden.

Note: The pastry can also be frozen for later use, or make double and freeze half for another time.

LAMB, RED ONION AND TZATZIKI FLATBREADS.

THESE ARE FRESH, FAST AND FABULOUS. PARTICULARLY IF YOU USE STORE-BOUGHT FLATBREADS.

SERVES 4 | PREPARATION TIME 10 minutes | COOKING TIME 15 minutes

WHAT YOU'LL NEED
LAMB
400 g lamb rump steak, deboned
salt and freshly ground black pepper
1 Tbsp olive oil or butter
2 whole cloves garlic
1 sprig fresh rosemary
4 pita breads (see page 58) or use store-bought pitas
1 small red onion, halved and finely sliced

WHAT TO DO
1. Season the lamb with salt and pepper. Heat a non-stick frying pan over medium-high heat and add the olive oil or butter. Add the lamb, whole garlic cloves and rosemary to the pan and fry for 4–5 minutes on each side, or until just cooked through and still pink in the middle. Remove from the heat and set aside on a board to rest for at least 5 minutes, then slice thinly on the diagonal.
2. Meanwhile, prepare your tzatziki (see below).
3. To serve, gently split open the pitas and add slivers of lamb, red onion and a dollop of tzatziki. Serve immediately.

Minty Tzatziki

SERVES 4 | PREPARATION TIME 5 minutes

WHAT YOU'LL NEED
½ cucumber, halved lengthways and deseeded
¾ cup double-thick natural yoghurt
½ clove garlic, minced
zest of ½ lemon
2 tsp lemon juice
1 Tbsp chopped fresh mint
salt and freshly ground black pepper to taste

WHAT TO DO
1. Finely dice the cucumber and mix with the remaining ingredients. Refrigerate until ready to serve.

Note: This meal is delicious served with a small Greek salad on the side.

OUR ULTIMATE OXTAIL.

IT'S HARDLY REVOLUTIONARY, BUT I GREW UP ON MANY STEAMING BOWLS OF SLOW, SLOW COOKED OXTAIL AND IT'S ONE OF MY FAVOURITE COMFORT FOODS. THIS IS HOW I MAKE IT AT HOME WHEN IT'S WONDERFULLY WINTERY OUTSIDE. SAVE ON CARBS AND SERVE WITH DELICIOUSLY CREAMY CAULIFLOWER MASH, BUT IT'S ALSO RICH AND ROBUST ENOUGH TO HAVE ON ITS OWN, OR WITH FRESH STEAMED GREENS ON THE SIDE.

SERVES 4 | PREPARATION TIME 10 minutes | COOKING TIME 3½ hours (mostly unattended)

WHAT YOU'LL NEED

1 Tbsp olive oil

1 Tbsp butter

1 kg oxtail, cut into pieces

1 large onion, chopped

1 large carrot, chopped

2 sticks celery, chopped

3–4 sprigs fresh thyme or 1 tsp dried

1 sprig fresh rosemary or 1 tsp dried

1 clove garlic, minced

1 x 410 g can chopped, peeled tomatoes

1 Tbsp tomato ketchup

1 Tbsp Worcestershire sauce

2 tsp sugar, or more to taste

1 cup red wine (optional, additionally use extra stock) or stout

2 cups beef stock

½ tsp each salt and freshly ground black pepper

2 Tbsp chopped fresh parsley, for serving

WHAT TO DO

1. Preheat the oven to 140 °C.
2. Heat the olive oil and butter in a large ovenproof saucepan over medium heat. When the butter starts to foam, add half the oxtail and brown for 4–5 minutes on each side or until golden, and then remove and set aside. Add a little extra oil if necessary and repeat with the remaining meat, also removing to set aside.
3. Add the onion, carrot, celery and herbs to the saucepan and fry for 5 minutes, or until the carrots and onions have softened slightly. Add the garlic and fry for another minute.
4. Add the canned tomatoes, ketchup and Worcestershire sauce, and sugar, and simmer for 10 minutes. Add the red wine or stout, the stock, as well as the oxtail and salt and black pepper, and bring the liquid to a slow boil. Remove the saucepan from the stovetop and place in the oven to cook for a further 3 hours, or until the meat falls away from the bones with no resistance. Add extra stock as you go along if at any point it becomes too dry. However, be careful not to add too much stock as you do want a luxuriously thick and rich sauce.
5. Check for seasoning, scatter over the parsley and serve. Alternatively, leave to cool, skim any fat off the surface and then reheat and serve. It tastes even better the next day once the flavours have had more time to mature.

Note: The meat and sauce is also gorgeous shredded into a ragû and served over ribbony slivers of pappardelle pasta.

SLOW-COOKED GOAT STEW
with Beery Dumplings.

I WILL NEVER FORGET THE FIRST TIME THAT I TASTED GOAT, ROASTED UNTIL CHARRED AT A ROADSIDE STALL IN VERY REMOTE NORTHERN KENYA. WE ATE SIMPLY, WITH OUR HANDS, AND HAD CREAMY SPICY CHAI (TEA) AFTERWARDS. IT WAS BEYOND DELICIOUS, AND THIS IS A TRIBUTE TO THAT.

SERVES 4–6 | PREPARATION TIME 10 minutes | FUSS-FREE COOKING TIME 1½–2 hours

WHAT YOU'LL NEED

GOAT STEW

2 Tbsp olive oil

800 g diced goat meat

2–3 sprigs fresh thyme or 1 tsp dried

1 sprig fresh rosemary or 1 tsp dried

1 medium-sized onion, chopped

1 fresh chilli, deseeded and chopped

2 cups chopped fresh tomatoes

1 large clove garlic, finely chopped

2 Tbsp tomato ketchup

1 Tbsp Worcestershire sauce

2 Tbsp chutney

1 cup chicken stock

salt and freshly ground black pepper

BEERY DUMPLINGS

200 g self-raising flour

50 g soft butter

½ cup grated Parmesan or cheese of
   your choice

2 Tbsp natural yoghurt

1 tsp chopped fresh rosemary

5 Tbsp beer

generous pinch each of salt and freshly
   ground black pepper

WHAT TO DO

1. Preheat the oven to 150 °C.
2. For the stew, heat the olive oil in a medium-sized ovenproof pan or skillet over medium-high heat. Fry the goat meat until golden on both sides, about 3–4 minutes per side. Remove the meat from the pan and set aside.
3. Add the thyme, rosemary, onion and chilli to the same pan and leave to cook on medium-low heat for 10 minutes, or until the onion has softened and is translucent. Add the chopped tomatoes, garlic, tomato ketchup, Worcestershire sauce and chutney and cook for another minute.
4. Return the meat to the pan and place in the oven for 1½–2 hours, adding in the stock and maybe a little water as you need to. Season with salt and pepper.
5. Meanwhile, for the dumplings, mix the flour and butter together (by hand or using a food processor) until the texture resembles breadcrumbs. Add the remaining dumpling ingredients and knead into a soft dough. If the dough is too wet add in a little more flour; it should not stick to your hands excessively. Roll palm-sized balls and place on top of the stew mixture. Bake without the lid for 6–10 minutes or until puffy and golden.

Note: Swop out goat for lamb if you prefer, or if goat meat is unavailable.

OSTRICH SKEWERS
with Red Onion, Roasted Butternut and Creamy Whipped Feta.

THESE OSTRICH KEBABS ARE UNFUSSY, OH-SO-PRETTY AND DOWNRIGHT DELICIOUS, WHICH MEANS THAT YOU'LL HAVE A VERITABLE PARTY IN YOUR MOUTH WHEN YOU MAKE THEM.

SERVES 4 | PREPARATION TIME 15 minutes | COOKING TIME 20 minutes

WHAT YOU'LL NEED

8 thin bamboo skewers
400 g butternut, peeled and cut into
   2 cm cubes
2 apples, cut into 2 cm cubes
500 g ostrich meat, cut into 2 cm cubes
   (or any red meat)
1 large red onion, quartered and separated
   into 'leaves'
salt and freshly ground black pepper
Creamy Whipped Feta (see page 64)

WHAT TO DO

1. Soak the bamboo skewers in water for 20 minutes to prevent them burning when cooking.
2. Meanwhile, cook the butternut cubes for 10 minutes, or until just cooked but still firm, in a medium-sized saucepan filled halfway with salted boiling water. Add the cubed apple for the last 3 minutes of the cooking time.
3. Assemble the kebabs by alternating cubes of ostrich, onion, apple and butternut onto each skewer. Brush with a little extra olive oil and season with salt and pepper.
4. Heat a frying pan over medium-high heat (or prepare your braai or bbq) and cook the kebabs for 4–5 minutes on each side, or until cooked through. Serve the kebabs immediately with the whipped feta, and pita breads (see page 58), if you like.

PORK CHOPS
with Pears, Cider and Mustard.

SERVES 4 | PREPARATION TIME 10 minutes | COOKING TIME 30 minutes

WHAT YOU'LL NEED

4 good-sized pork chops

generous pinch of salt and freshly ground
  black pepper

1–2 Tbsp olive oil

1 Tbsp butter

1 large red onion, roughly chopped

2 pears, cored and roughly chopped

1 sprig fresh rosemary or ½ tsp dried

½ cup cider

⅓ cup fresh cream or double-thick yoghurt

2 tsp Dijon mustard

WHAT TO DO

1. Season the meat with salt and pepper on both sides. Heat the olive oil in a large pan over a medium-high heat, and brown the meat for 4–5 minutes on each side until golden and no longer pink in the middle. Using kitchen tongs, stand the chops upright to cook and crisp up the rind for an extra 1–2 minutes. Remove the meat and set aside on a warmed serving platter.

2. Heat the butter in the same pan and gently fry the red onion and pears, along with the rosemary, until lightly golden and softened, 8–10 minutes. Remove and add to the resting meat.

3. Pour the cider into the pan and simmer for a further 10 minutes, or until it reduces slightly and starts to thicken. Add the cream or yoghurt and stir through the mustard. Simmer for another 4–5 minutes, check for seasoning and adjust accordingly, and then pour the whole mixture over the chops and rest until serving.

Notes: Serve with just-cooked green beans and cauliflower or sweet potato mash.

This works just as well with good old pork bangers, or with skin-on chicken thighs.

ROAST LEG OF LAMB
with Minty Gremolata and Gravy.

ROAST LAMB HAS ALWAYS BEEN A SPECIAL MEAL IN MY FAMILY, PARTLY BECAUSE LAMB ISN'T ALL THAT EASY TO COME BY IN ZIMBABWE, SO WE'D EAT IT WHEN ON HOLIDAY IN CAPE TOWN (ALONG WITH MY MUM'S INCREDIBLE LAMB STEW). I'VE ADDED A LOUDLY FRESH AND BRIGHT GREMOLATA (SIMILAR TO PESTO) IN THIS CASE, JUST TO ADD A LITTLE EXTRA SOMETHING.

SERVES 4–6 | PREPARATION TIME 10 minutes | COOKING TIME 1½ hours (mostly unattended)

WHAT YOU'LL NEED

LAMB
1.75 kg leg of lamb
3 cloves garlic, halved
1 clove garlic, crushed
1 Tbsp finely chopped fresh rosemary
juice and zest of 1 lemon
2 Tbsp butter
2 Tbsp olive oil
generous pinch each of salt and freshly
   ground black pepper

MINTY GREMOLATA
4 cloves garlic, crushed
½ cup chopped fresh parsley
¼ cup chopped fresh mint
¼ cup lemon juice
zest of 2 large lemons
2 tsp sea salt flakes
¼–½ cup good-quality olive oil

WHAT TO DO

1. Remove the lamb from the fridge at least 1 hour before cooking so that it can come to room temperature. Before you are ready to start cooking, preheat the oven to 200 °C.
2. Set aside the halved garlic cloves and then mix together the remaining ingredients for the lamb until you have a paste.
3. Randomly cut slits into the lamb with a small sharp knife and insert half a garlic clove into each one, then baste the entire leg with the rosemary paste.
4. Roast for 1 hour 10 minutes (for medium-rare), and then remove from the oven and leave to rest, covered with tinfoil, for at least 15 minutes.
5. While the lamb rests, prepare the gremolata by blitzing all the ingredients together in a food processor or use a pestle and mortar.
6. Carve the lamb and serve immediately with the gremolata.

Note: You can also make an easy gravy with the pan juices by adding in 1 Tbsp cake flour, 100 ml red wine (optional) and about 1 cup stock. Whisk and simmer gently until the gravy thickens to the consistency you prefer.

LAMB AND LENTIL BOBOTIE.

BOBOTIE IS A FAIRLY EPIC SOUTH AFRICAN FAVOURITE, ROOTED IN DUTCH AND CAPE MALAY ORIGINS AND LAYERED WITH MILD CURRIED FLAVOURS AND TOPPED WITH A SIMPLE EGG CUSTARD. IT'S HEROIC COMFORT FOOD.

SERVES 4–6 | PREPARATION TIME 20 minutes | COOKING TIME 35–40 minutes

WHAT YOU'LL NEED

2 slices wholewheat bread
1 Tbsp olive oil
1 Tbsp butter
500 g lamb mince
2 medium-sized onions, chopped
1 clove garlic, minced
1 apple, peeled, cored and grated
1 tsp grated fresh ginger
2 tsp medium curry powder
1 tsp ground coriander
1 tsp turmeric
½ tsp ground cinnamon
½ tsp dried chilli flakes
½ tsp each of dried mixed herbs
1 Tbsp chutney
salt and freshly ground black pepper
1 Tbsp lemon juice
½ cup seedless raisins
1 x 400 g can lentils, drained
2 Tbsp flaked almonds
2 bay leaves

BAKED EGG TOPPING

1 cup milk
½ tsp salt
pinch of freshly ground black pepper
2 eggs

WHAT TO DO

1. Preheat the oven to 190 °C and grease an ovenproof dish well. I prefer a slightly smaller dish that makes a deeper, moister bobotie.
2. Soak the bread in water.
2. Heat the oil and butter in a pan on medium-high heat and fry the mince, stirring often until loose and crumbly. Add the onions and fry until soft and translucent.
3. Add the garlic, apple, ginger, spices, herbs and chutney and cook for another minute. Season with salt, pepper and lemon juice. Lightly squeeze the bread and then mash it with a fork. Add the mashed bread, raisins, lentils and almonds to the bobotie mixture.
4. Spread the mixture in the ovenproof dish and insert the bay leaves.
5. Beat all the ingredients for the topping with a fork and pour over the top.
6. Bake uncovered for 30–35 minutes, or until the custard topping is firm and golden brown.

poultry.

SUMMERY POACHED CHICKEN
with Smashed Lemony Peas.

THIS IS LIGHT AND FRESH AND BURSTING WITH ALL MANNER OF SPRINGTIME LOVELINESS.

SERVES 4 | PREPARATION TIME 10 minutes | COOKING TIME 10–15 minutes

WHAT YOU'LL NEED
4 cups (1 L) good-quality chicken stock
4 skinless chicken breasts

LEMONY PEAS
2 cups peas (I use frozen) OR 1 cup peas
   and 1 cup shelled broad beans
1 Tbsp lemon juice
1 tsp lemon zest
1 Tbsp olive oil, plus extra for drizzling
1–2 tsp chopped fresh mint, plus extra
   leaves for garnishing
salt and freshly ground black pepper
Parmesan shavings, for serving

WHAT TO DO
1. Bring the chicken stock to a boil and add the chicken breasts. Turn the heat down so that the stock is at a gentle simmer, and poach for 8–10 minutes, or until the chicken breasts have just cooked through. Don't overcook as they will become tough.
2. Meanwhile, cook the peas for 1–2 minutes in salted boiling water, drain, mash and add the remaining ingredients.
3. Slice the chicken on the diagonal into 1-cm-thick slices. Serve immediately in warmed bowls on a bed of smashed peas, with a drizzle of olive oil, some Parmesan shavings and a few fresh mint leaves.

ROSEMARY AND MUSTARD CHICKEN BREASTS.

THIS IS A MID-WEEK CRACKER. THE ULTIMATE DELIVERER OF BANG-FOR-YOUR-BUCK IN TERMS OF FUSS-FREE FLAVOUR.

SERVES 4 | PREPARATION TIME 10 minutes | COOKING TIME 15 minutes

WHAT YOU'LL NEED

4 plump chicken breasts, skin on
salt and freshly ground black pepper
1 Tbsp olive oil or butter
2 whole cloves garlic
1 sprig fresh rosemary
2 tsp Dijon mustard
¼ cup chicken stock or white wine
¼ cup fresh cream (optional, alternatively
    add a little more stock)
1 cup frozen peas
1 Tbsp lemon juice, for serving
1 heaped tsp lemon zest, for serving
fresh parsley, for serving

WHAT TO DO

1. Season the chicken breasts lightly with salt and pepper.
2. To a large pan over medium-high heat, add the olive oil or butter and, when hot (or the butter starts to foam), add the chicken breasts, skin-side down, and cook for 3–4 minutes, or until the skin is golden and crispy. Cook for 2–3 minutes on the other side, then remove the breasts from the pan and set aside.
3. Add the garlic cloves and rosemary sprig to the same pan and cook for about a minute, then add the mustard, stock or white wine and cream (or more stock) – this will pick up all the sticky caramelised bits from the base of the pan, which is where all the flavour will be (it's called 'deglazing the pan'). Simmer for 2–3 minutes or until the sauce starts to thicken slightly, then return the breasts to the pan for another 3–4 minutes. Remove the pan from the heat, stir through the frozen peas until heated through and set aside to rest for a few minutes before serving.
4. Serve with a drizzle of lemon juice, a scattering of lemon zest and fresh parsley.

Note: Serve with a creamy sweet potato or cauliflower mash, or with extra greens such as baby spinach and tenderstem broccoli or mange tout.

QUICK CHICKEN BIRYANI.

WE CAN'T ESCAPE OUR CURRY HERITAGE HERE IN SOUTH AFRICA, AND I AM NOT COMPLAINING. AND AS IS SO OFTEN THE CASE WITH A GOOD CURRY OR INDIAN DISH THAT REQUIRES LOTS OF LOVE AND LAYERING OF FLAVOURS, THE INGREDIENTS LIST IS FAIRLY LONG, BUT THE INPUT IS EXCEPTIONALLY EXCEEDED BY THE OUTPUT THAT DELIVERS A BEAUTIFULLY FLUFFY AND FRAGRANT CURRIED RICE DISH THAT YOU CAN'T HELP BUT FALL IN LOVE WITH.

SERVES 4 | PREPARATION TIME 10 minutes | COOKING TIME 25 minutes

WHAT YOU'LL NEED

1 cup basmati rice

2 Tbsp cooking oil

1 large onion, finely chopped

1 heaped tsp grated fresh ginger

750 g skinless chicken breast fillets, cut into 2 cm cubes and lightly seasoned

2 cloves garlic, minced

1 Tbsp medium curry powder (or mild if you prefer)

1 tsp each of ground coriander, turmeric and ground cumin

3 cardamom pods, 'bruised' to crack them open

1 cinnamon stick or $\frac{1}{2}$ tsp ground cinnamon

$\frac{1}{2}$ cup dried apricots, roughly chopped

$\frac{1}{2}$ cup seedless raisins

$\frac{1}{4}$ cup toasted slivered almonds, for serving

roughly torn or chopped fresh coriander, for serving

$\frac{1}{2}$ cup natural yoghurt or buttermilk with 1 Tbsp chopped fresh mint stirred through, to serve on the side

WHAT TO DO

1. Cook the rice according to the packet instructions in lightly salted boiling water, then drain and set aside.

2. Meanwhile, to a large saucepan over medium heat, add the cooking oil and gently fry the onion for 4–5 minutes, or until softened. Add the ginger and chicken and cook for another 4 minutes, stirring occasionally.

3. Add the garlic and spices and cook for a minute, stirring well to coat all the chicken.

4. Add the cooked rice along with the apricots and raisins, place the lid on the saucepan but turn off the heat and leave to steam for another 5 minutes before serving immediately with a scattering of toasted slivered almonds and coriander, as well as the minted yoghurt or buttermilk on the side.

FIERY CHICKEN LIVERS
with Cauliflower Mash.

SPICY CHICKEN LIVERS ARE SERVED IN MANY CORNERS OF AFRICA, AND MOST FAMOUSLY IN MOZAMBIQUE. SERVE WITH FRESH PORTUGUESE BREAD *(PÃO)* OR CREAMY CAULIFLOWER MASH LIKE I'VE SHOWN HERE.

SERVES 4 | PREPARATION TIME 10 minutes | COOKING TIME 25 minutes

WHAT YOU'LL NEED

1 Tbsp butter

1 Tbsp olive oil

400 g fresh chicken livers

1 small onion or shallot, finely chopped

100 g bacon, chopped

1 fresh chilli, deseeded and finely chopped

1 tsp paprika

2–3 sprigs fresh thyme

1 clove garlic, minced

100 ml chicken stock

1 Tbsp tomato ketchup

1 x 410 g can peeled, chopped tomatoes

2 tsp light brown sugar

$\frac{1}{4}$–$\frac{1}{2}$ cup fresh cream

$\frac{1}{2}$ tsp each of salt and freshly ground
   black pepper

2 Tbsp chopped fresh parsley, for serving

CAULIFLOWER MASH

2 medium heads cauliflower, roughly
   chopped

1 Tbsp butter

1 Tbsp olive oil

$\frac{1}{4}$ cup milk to loosen, if necessary

salt and freshly ground black pepper

WHAT TO DO

1. For the livers, heat the butter and olive oil over medium-high heat in a heavy-based pan. Fry the livers for 3–4 minutes, remove from the pan with a slotted spoon and drain on kitchen paper.

2. Reduce the heat to medium, add the onion or shallot, bacon, chilli, paprika and thyme and cook for 8–10 minutes, or until the onion has softened. Add the garlic for the last minute.

3. Add the stock, ketchup, tomatoes, sugar, cream and seasoning and simmer for 5 minutes. Return the chicken livers to the pan and simmer for a further 15 minutes.

4. Meanwhile, steam the cauliflower until soft, then mix together with the butter, olive oil, a little milk and salt and pepper. Blend until smooth using a stick blender, adding extra milk if needed.

5. Serve the livers spooned over the cauliflower mash and top with a sprinkling of fresh parsley.

Note: To serve as a snack or for a variation, serve the livers bruschetta-style on fresh ciabatta toasts, with a sprinkling of fresh parsley.

QUICK CAJUN CHICKEN WRAPS
with Avocado Mayonnaise.

A CAJUN SPICE MIX IS A BLEND OF NATIVE AMERICAN, FRENCH, SPANISH AND AFRICAN FLAVOURS THAT'S UNIQUE TO THE US STATE OF LOUISIANA. IT'S FIERY AND PACKED FULL OF FLAVOUR AND ON THE WHOLE, PRETTY AMAZING. IT'S ALSO A WAY TO DRESS UP A FAIRLY ORDINARY SET OF CHICKEN STRIPS AND TURN THEM INTO SOMETHING WORTH HAVING A PARTY FOR. CAJUN FOOD EMBODIES A LOT THAT I LOVE WHEN IT COMES TO FOOD – IT'S ABOUT COOKING SIMPLE, EATING LOCAL AND MAKING SURE THERE'S ENOUGH TO SHARE. THE PREDOMINANT SEASONINGS (AND AS ALWAYS, OPINIONS VARY HERE) ARE OREGANO, THYME, CAYENNE PEPPER, PAPRIKA, GROUND CUMIN AND OFTEN MUSTARD, ONION OR GARLIC POWDER.

SERVES 4 | PREPARATION TIME 10 minutes | COOKING TIME 10 minutes

WHAT YOU'LL NEED

2 skinless chicken breasts, sliced lengthways

salt and freshly ground black pepper

mixture of $\frac{1}{2}$ tsp each of ground cumin, ground coriander, sweet paprika and dried thyme (or use a pre-mixed Cajun seasoning)

1 Tbsp olive oil

1 whole sweetcorn on the cob (optional)

4 tortilla wraps

$\frac{1}{2}$ cup Avocado Mayonnaise (see Note)

fresh salad greens, for serving

1 lemon, quartered

WHAT TO DO

1. Season the chicken breasts and then generously coat them in the Cajun spice mix. Heat the olive oil in a nonstick pan and fry the chicken breasts for 2–3 minutes on each side, or until golden and cooked through.
2. Remove from the heat, set aside and slice into 1 cm slivers on the diagonal.
3. In the same pan, chargrill the sweetcorn in a little olive oil and then slice off the kernels (if using).
4. Wipe the pan clean and heat the wraps for about 45 seconds on each side. Lay flat, spread with about 1 Tbsp avocado mayonnaise, scatter over a few fresh greens and top with the chicken slices. Squeeze over a little lemon juice and serve immediately.

Note: To make the Avocado Mayo, place 1 egg, $\frac{1}{2}$ clove garlic (optional), $\frac{1}{2}$ depipped and peeled avocado, juice of 1 lemon or lime, small handful fresh basil leaves (optional), and pinch each of salt and black pepper in a blender. Turn on the blender and then slowly drizzle in $\frac{3}{4}$ cup cooking oil (not olive oil). It should emulsify and thicken to the usual consistency of mayonnaise within a minute.

BARBECUED CHICKEN.

THERE'S LITTLE THAT WE LOVE MORE IN AFRICA THAN A FLAME-GRILLED CHICKEN. ADD TO THAT OUR VERY SOUTH AFRICAN CHAKALAKA AND YOU'RE IN FOR A FEAST.

SERVES 4 | PREPARATION TIME 10 minutes | COOKING TIME 30–35 minutes

WHAT YOU'LL NEED

BBQ SAUCE

2 Tbsp olive oil

2 Tbsp tomato ketchup

2 Tbsp balsamic vinegar

1 Tbsp runny honey

1 Tbsp lemon juice

1 fresh chilli, deseeded and chopped,
    or 1 tsp dried chilli flakes

2 tsp paprika

½ tsp dried coriander

½ tsp ground cinnamon

2 cloves garlic, minced

generous pinch each of salt and freshly
    ground black pepper

CHICKEN

1 whole spatchcock-style chicken or
    8 mixed chicken pieces, skin on

chakalaka relish, for serving

WHAT TO DO

1. Combine all the bbq sauce ingredients in a jug.
2. Baste the chicken with the sauce, cover with clingfilm and leave to stand in the fridge for as long as possible before cooking (overnight is ideal, but not essential). Remove from the fridge and bring to room temperature about 20 minutes before cooking.
3. Cook on the barbecue for 30–35 minutes, with the lid down if you have one, turning halfway, until cooked through. Baste with any extra sauce every 10 minutes or so during cooking.
4. Serve immediately with a spicy chakalaka relish, a side salad or a generous spoonful of mealie pap or polenta.

Note: To turn a whole chicken into a flattie, place the chicken so that the drumsticks are on top. Cut all the way along the breastbone with kitchen scissors (most recipes recommend cutting down the breastbone, but I find this much easier). Pull the chicken apart and lay it flat on a roasting tray.

DUKKAH-CRUSTED CHICKEN
with White Bean and Olive Oil Mash.

SERVES 4 | PREPARATION TIME 5–10 minutes | COOKING TIME 10 minutes

WHAT YOU'LL NEED

4 skinless chicken breasts

2 Tbsp dukkah spice rub

about 3 Tbsp olive oil

2 x 410 g cans cannellini beans, drained

salt and freshly ground black pepper

squeeze of lemon juice, for serving

fresh parsley leaves, for garnishing

WHAT TO DO

1. Slice the chicken breasts in half along the middle (so that they make two very thin breasts; basically 'butterfly' them all the way through). Sprinkle each piece with a generous coating of dukkah rub.

2. Heat a frying pan on medium-high heat, add 1 Tbsp olive oil and fry the chicken breasts for 3–4 minutes on each side, or until golden and cooked through. Remove from the pan and set aside to rest.

3. While the chicken rests, heat the cannellini beans in a small saucepan, season to taste with salt and pepper, add a drizzle of olive oil (about 2 Tbsp) and mash roughly. Add 1–2 Tbsp warm water to loosen if necessary.

4. Serve the chicken and mash immediately with a drizzle of lemon juice and a scattering of fresh parsley.

Note: This bean mash is arguably lower in calories than ordinary mashed potato, which you could also certainly use. Alternatively, use sweet potatoes, or cauliflower mash, or just serve with fresh steamed greens for a lighter option.

SPANISH-STYLE ROAST CHICKEN
with Chorizo and Blistered Lemons.

YOU COULD ALMOST CALL THIS YOUR IDEAL 'SPRINGTIME SPANISH-STYLE ROAST CHICKEN' BECAUSE IT HOLDS THE DELIGHTFUL PROMISE OF CHILLED SANGRIA AND SUNNY DAYS WITH TIME ON YOUR HANDS AND FOOD ON THE GO. IT'S GOT ALL THE FLAIR AND FLAVOUR AND COLOUR THAT YOU'D EXPECT FROM ANY SPANISH-STYLE FIESTA FOOD, BUT IT'S ALSO LIGHT ENOUGH AND RELAXED ENOUGH TO BE PERFECT LAID-BACK SHARING FOOD. ALSO, IT HAS THE (MASSIVE) ADDED BONUS OF ALL BEING COOKED UP IN ONE DISH. A SIMPLE ASSEMBLAGE OF INGREDIENTS AND YOU'RE JUST A FOOT-TAP AWAY FROM GLORIOUS CHICKEN-Y CHORIZO-Y BLISTERED LEMON GLORY.

SERVES 4 | PREPARATION TIME 5 minutes | COOKING TIME 45–60 minutes

WHAT YOU'LL NEED

about 400 g baby potatoes, skin on

100 g good-quality chorizo, thinly sliced

2 red onions, peeled and cut into sixths

4 cloves garlic, peeled but left whole

2 sprigs fresh rosemary

4 sprigs fresh thyme

8–10 chicken pieces, skin on

olive oil for coating

1 tsp smoked paprika

generous pinch each of salt and freshly ground black pepper

2 lemons, quartered

WHAT TO DO

1. Preheat the oven to 180 °C.
2. Add all the ingredients, except the lemons, to a large roasting dish. Toss everything gently to coat evenly in the olive oil and paprika. Season well with salt and pepper and then add the lemon quarters.
3. Roast uncovered for 25–30 minutes, or until the chicken is just cooked through and the juices run clear when you insert a knife into the flesh. Remove the chicken, drain the pan juices into a small saucepan to make gravy, and return the potatoes etc. to the oven to crisp up a little while the chicken rests.
4. Serve immediately with the gravy made from the pan juices.

Notes: To make a quick gravy, take the pan juices plus gravy powder and mix together, adding hot water according to packet instructions. Simmer gently until the mixture thickens slightly. You could also squeeze in the juice of some of the blistered lemons for extra flavour if you like. For a spicy rosé sangria, mix together 1 x 750 ml bottle rosé wine, 1 cup fresh orange juice, juice of 1 lime, 2 cups lemonade or ginger ale, 1 cup soda water, 1 sliced and depipped peach or nectarine, 1 cinnamon stick and a handful of fresh mint leaves. Serve over plenty of ice.

QUICK HONEY CITRUS DUCK
with French Beans and Toasted Almonds.

ROB AND I WERE LUCKY ENOUGH TO EAT DUCK IN PARIS WHEN WE WERE THERE ON HONEYMOON. IN FACT, THERE WAS A PARTICULAR RESTAURANT WITH A PARTICULARLY DELICIOUS CITRUSY DUCK DISH THAT WE WENT BACK TO THREE TIMES IN TWO DAYS. THIS IS A LITTLE NOD TO THAT, AND I HOPE YOU LIKE IT.

SERVES 4 | PREPARATION TIME 5–10 minutes | COOKING TIME 25 minutes

WHAT YOU'LL NEED

2 duck breasts
salt and freshly ground black pepper

CITRUS SYRUP
zest and juice of 1 orange or clementine
zest of 1 lemon
2 Tbsp honey
1–2 tsp grated fresh ginger
½ tsp each of ground cinnamon and
   nutmeg

GREEN BEANS AND ALMONDS
250 g green beans, topped and tailed
2 tsp olive oil
squeeze of lemon juice
small handful roasted almonds, roughly
   chopped

WHAT TO DO

1. Preheat the oven to 200 °C.
2. Season the duck breasts with salt and pepper. Add the duck breasts to a heavy-based pan (preferably ovenproof) over medium-high heat and brown skin-side down for 5–6 minutes, or until golden. Cook on the other side for about 2 minutes.
3. Stir all the syrup ingredients together in a bowl. Leave the duck breasts in the pan or transfer to an ovenproof baking dish, add the citrus syrup and roast for a further 5–8 minutes in the oven, or until the juices run clear. Remove and allow to rest for 5 minutes.
4. While the duck rests, simmer the sauce over a medium-low heat to reduce and thicken a little more so that it's nice and sticky.
5. Cook the beans in salted boiling water for 1–2 minutes, drain, drizzle with the olive oil and lemon juice and scatter over the chopped almonds.
6. Slice the duck thinly and serve with the green beans and a drizzle of the citrus syrup.

Notes: Also works with duck legs, though the roasting time may vary by 5–10 minutes.
You could also serve this with crispy roast potatoes or cauliflower mash (see page 101).

pasta.

ROAST CHICKEN AND PEA LASAGNE
with Ricotta and Lemon.

SERVES 4 | PREPARATION TIME 10 minutes | COOKING TIME 35–40 minutes (mostly unattended)

WHAT YOU'LL NEED

½ Tbsp olive oil
100 g baby spinach
2 cups frozen peas
250 g ricotta cheese
200 g smooth cottage cheese
1 tsp lemon zest
1 Tbsp lemon juice
1–2 Tbsp milk, to loosen
2 cups shredded roast chicken meat
½ cup grated Parmesan or pecorino
    cheese, or use mature Cheddar
salt and freshly ground black pepper
9–12 sheets lasagne
1 cup grated mozzarella cheese

WHAT TO DO

1. Preheat the oven to 200 °C and grease a 20 x 25 cm baking dish.
2. To a large frying pan over medium heat, add the olive oil and then the spinach and peas. Cook for 2–3 minutes or until the spinach wilts, then remove from the heat and set aside in a sieve, so that any excess liquid from the spinach can drain away.
3. In a large mixing bowl, mix together the ricotta and cottage cheese, along with the lemon zest and juice. Add the milk to loosen, if necessary. Add the chicken, cheese and seasoning and mix until combined.
4. Layer the ingredients in the baking dish as follows: a layer of filling, a layer of lasagne sheets. Continue layering the two and then end with a final layer of filling on the top. Top with the grated mozzarella and bake for 25–30 minutes, or until golden and bubbling and the pasta sheets are cooked through and can be easily pierced with a knife.

ROASTED BUTTERNUT AND RICOTTA RAVIOLI
with Sage Butter.

YES, I KNOW, THIS IS HARDLY A REVOLUTIONARY RECIPE, BUT OH MY GOODNESS IS IT INCREDIBLE TO EAT. THE CREAMY FILLING OF ROASTED BUTTERNUT AND LIGHT, FLUFFY RICOTTA IS OFFSET PERFECTLY BY THE NUTTY GOLDEN SAGE BUTTER. IT'S ALSO A FABULOUS ALMOST-FANCY BUT UNFUSSY CROWD PLEASER THAT CAN MOSTLY BE MADE IN ADVANCE. ALSO, IT'S A HUMBLE NOD TO ITALY, WHERE THE OTHER ME MOST SURELY LIVES. I ADORE THEIR EXQUISITELY SIMPLE APPROACH TO FOOD, AND EVERY VISIT SENDS ME HOME LOOKING BACK OVER MY SHOULDER.

SERVES 4 | PREPARATION TIME approx. 30 minutes | COOKING TIME 5–10 minutes

WHAT YOU'LL NEED

BUTTERNUT FILLING
400 g butternut, peeled and cubed

2 Tbsp olive oil

salt and freshly ground black pepper

small pinch of ground nutmeg

100 g ricotta, roughly crumbled

100 g pecorino or Parmesan cheese, grated
   or shaved, for serving

PASTA
300 g cake flour, plus a little extra for
   dusting

3 large eggs

½ tsp salt

SAGE BUTTER
100 g butter

2 Tbsp extra-virgin olive oil

2–3 sage leaves, roughly torn

WHAT TO DO

1. Preheat the oven to 200 °C.
2. Place the butternut in a large roasting tin and drizzle with the olive oil, then toss gently to coat and season with salt, pepper and a sprinkling of nutmeg. Roast for 20–25 minutes, or until golden and it can be easily pierced with a knife.
3. Meanwhile, prepare the pasta by adding the flour to a large mixing bowl or food processor. Add the eggs and salt and mix well until it forms a ball, then knead on a lightly floured surface for 3–5 minutes, or until silky and smooth. Wrap in clingfilm and leave to rest and chill in the fridge for 15–20 minutes.
4. Blend the butternut and ricotta together in a food processor until smooth. Remove, check for seasoning and set aside to cool.
5. Divide the pasta dough into four sections, returning the remaining three to the fridge in the clingfilm while you work with the first section. Roll the dough as thinly as possible, 1–2 mm thick, using a rolling pin or a pasta machine. If using a pasta machine, start on the thickest setting and then work your way down, folding the pasta sheet into three between each rolling (effectively folding it into thirds). When it's thin enough, dust the sheet lightly with flour and set aside, and continue to do the same with the remaining dough.
6. Use a 7–8 cm round or square fluted cutter, or large round cookie cutter of a similar size, and cut out as many circles as possible, it

should give you about 40. Divide the circles in half, keeping about 20 aside for the 'lids', and put a small tablespoon-ful of butternut and ricotta filling into the centre of the remaining 20. Brush around the edge with a little water and place a 'lid' on top, gently pressing out any excess air with your fingers before sealing.

7. To cook, add the ravioli in batches to a large pot of salted boiling water, removing with a slotted spoon when they rise to the surface (2–3 minutes). Set aside on a warmed serving platter drizzled with a little olive oil. Keep aside about ¼ cup cooking water to use later, if necessary.

8. To prepare the sage butter, add the butter and olive oil to a large frying pan over medium heat. Cook until the butter foams and takes on a light golden brown colour, then add the sage leaves and fry until they are crispy, a further 2–3 minutes. Take care not to let the butter burn.

9. Remove the pan from the heat and add the ravioli to the sage butter, mixing gently so that they are all well coated, and add in some of your pasta water to loosen, if necessary. Serve immediately with pecorino or Parmesan cheese scattered over the top.

Note: For a speedier version you can use wilted baby spinach instead of butternut; just squeeze out any excess water before blending together with the ricotta.

PRAWN AND SAFFRON SPAGHETTI.

OH, THIS IS PRETTY. THE RICH GOLDEN YELLOW OF THE SAFFRON LENDS A LITTLE *JE NE SAIS QUOI* TO THE DISH THAT CAN'T BE IGNORED, AND IT'S JUST A LITTLE FANCY. ALSO, IT'S A DOODLE TO MAKE AND YOU CAN BE FEASTING ON PLUMP PINK PRAWNS AND SILKY TWIRLS OF SPAGHETTI IN ABOUT 15 MINUTES. I'M LUCKY ENOUGH TO HAVE A LITTLE COLLECTION OF SPICES FROM ZANZIBAR, AND AMONG THEM ARE MY PRECIOUS SAFFRON THREADS, ADDED CAREFULLY TO SPECIAL DISHES TO GIVE THEM THAT GOLDEN GLOW THAT REMINDS ME SO MUCH OF THEIR SPICY, FRESH, COLOURFUL ISLAND FOOD.

SERVES 4 | PREPARATION TIME 10 minutes | COOKING TIME 15–20 minutes

WHAT YOU'LL NEED
pinch of saffron threads

100 ml hot fish or vegetable stock

400 g spaghetti or linguini

1 Tbsp olive oil, plus a dash extra

1 Tbsp butter

700–800 g prawns, deveined and shelled

1 large clove garlic, minced

1 small red chilli, deseeded and finely chopped

100 ml fresh cream (optional, alternatively use extra stock)

salt and freshly ground black pepper

Parmesan shavings, small handful roughly torn fresh basil leaves (or use parsley) and lemon wedges, for serving

fresh crusty bread, for serving (optional)

WHAT TO DO
1. Add the saffron threads to the hot stock to steep.
2. Cook the pasta in lots of salted boiling water along with a dash of olive oil. Drain, drizzle with extra olive oil and set aside.
3. Meanwhile, heat the 1 Tbsp olive oil and the butter in a large heavy-based saucepan over medium heat and add the prawns for 2 minutes, then add the garlic and chilli and fry for another minute or until the prawns turn pink. Add the stock and cream (if using), and remove from the heat.
4. Season to taste, then add the pasta to the pan and toss gently to combine everything.
5. Serve immediately in warmed bowls with Parmesan shavings, fresh basil or parsley, lemon wedges and fresh crusty bread on the side.

LINGUINI
with Chorizo and Chilli Calamari and Pea and Mint Pesto.

I LOVE THIS! PARTLY BECAUSE I AM MILDLY OBSESSED WITH CHORIZO AND ITS ABILITY TO TRANSPORT US ALL THE WAY TO THE MEDITERRANEAN, AND ALSO BECAUSE IT'S COMPLEMENTED SO BEAUTIFULLY BY THE PUNCHY, FRESH PEA AND MINT PESTO. OH, AND ALSO BECAUSE THE SAUCE MAKES ITSELF SO VERY AT HOME IN ITS BED OF LINGUINI, AND ONE OF MY VERY FAVOURITE THINGS TO DO IS TWIRL PASTA AROUND A FORK AND GOBBLE IT GREEDILY.

SERVES 4 | PREPARATION TIME 5 minutes | COOKING TIME 10–12 minutes

WHAT YOU'LL NEED

400 g linguini or spaghetti

2 Tbsp olive oil, plus extra for drizzling

500 g fresh calamari rings

½–1 tsp dried chilli flakes

generous pinch each of salt and freshly ground black pepper

100 g chorizo, cubed

fresh mint and Parmesan shavings, for garnishing

PEA AND MINT PESTO

1 heaped cup frozen peas, thawed

2 Tbsp grated Parmesan cheese

2 Tbsp roasted almonds

½ clove garlic, crushed

½ small green chilli, deseeded and finely chopped (optional)

1–2 Tbsp olive oil

1 Tbsp lemon juice

1 Tbsp chopped fresh mint

pinch of salt and freshly ground black pepper, or more to taste

1–2 Tbsp hot water to loosen, if necessary

WHAT TO DO

1. Cook the pasta in salted boiling water with 1 Tbsp olive oil until al dente. Drain, drizzle with a little more olive oil and set aside.

2. Meanwhile, blitz together all the pesto ingredients, check for seasoning, loosen with a little olive oil or hot water if necessary, and set aside.

3. Rinse the calamari rings, drain in a colander and set aside on a plate lined with kitchen paper or a clean dishcloth to dry off. The drier the squid, the crispier the end result. Season with the chilli flakes and salt and pepper.

4. Heat the remaining olive oil in a frying pan or wok. Add the chorizo and fry for 2–3 minutes, then add the calamari and cook for 3–4 minutes, or until lightly golden and crispy.

5. Toss together the pasta and pesto, sprinkle over the chorizo, calamari, mint leaves and Parmesan shavings and serve immediately in warmed bowls.

BAKED PUMPKIN RISOTTO
with Goat's Cheese and Sage.

PUMPKIN IS A FAVOURITE IN ZIMBABWE, AND I LOVE FINDING NEW WAYS TO COOK WITH IT. AND SO WHY ON EARTH WOULDN'T I HEAD DOWN A ROAD FILLED WITH GLORIOUSLY CREAMY RISOTTO DOTTED WITH GOAT'S CHEESE AND JUST A HINT OF SAGE?

SERVES 4 | PREPARATION TIME 15–20 minutes | COOKING TIME 30 minutes

WHAT YOU'LL NEED

2 cups peeled and cubed pumpkin (use ready-peeled and cut, if you like)

olive oil, for drizzling

salt and freshly ground black pepper

2 Tbsp olive oil

2 Tbsp butter

1 medium-sized onion, peeled and finely chopped

1 clove garlic, chopped

1 Tbsp chopped fresh sage or 1 tsp dried

1 cup Arborio (risotto) rice

½ cup white wine

700 ml chicken or vegetable stock

⅓ cup grated pecorino cheese (or Parmesan or Gruyère), plus extra for serving

½ cup goat's cheese (or use feta or Gorgonzola)

dollop of crème fraîche, for serving

WHAT TO DO

1. Preheat the oven to 180 °C.
2. Place the pumpkin in an ovenproof dish, drizzle with olive oil and sprinkle with salt and pepper. Bake for 15–20 minutes or until soft and it can be easily pierced with a knife. Remove from the oven and purée half of it.
3. Heat the 2 Tbsp olive oil and the butter in an ovenproof pan and fry the onion until softened, about 7 minutes. Add the garlic, half the sage and the risotto rice, stirring until well coated with oil. Pour in the wine and simmer for 5 minutes.
4. Stir well and add the stock. Cover and cook in the oven for 15–20 minutes or until the rice is soft but still al dente.
5. Remove from the oven and vigorously stir in in the pecorino, Parmesan or Gruyère until the risotto is creamy. Add the pumpkin purée and scatter over the goat's cheese, feta or Gorgonzola and the remaining cubed pumpkin and sage.
6. Serve immediately with a few extra pecorino shavings, as well as a dollop of crème fraîche.

WILD MUSHROOM GNOCCHI.

THIS RECIPE IS A VERSION OF THE ONE THAT I COOKED IN THE FIRST SEASON OF MY TV SHOW WITH OUR ADORED SOUTH AFRICAN–FRENCH CHEF FRANCK DANGEREUX. I REMEMBER PANICKING AT THE TIME AND ASKING MYSELF 'WHAT WAS I THINKING SERVING SOMETHING SO RIDICULOUSLY SIMPLE TO ONE OF THE BEST CHEFS IN THE COUNTRY' – BUT THEN I'LL NEVER FORGET HIS EMPTY PLATE AFTERWARDS.

SERVES 4 | PREPARATION TIME 5 minutes | COOKING TIME 10 minutes

WHAT YOU'LL NEED

1 Tbsp butter

1 Tbsp olive oil , plus extra for drizzling and serving

400 g mixed mushrooms, roughly chopped or torn

1 clove garlic, finely chopped

1 sprig fresh rosemary

1–2 Tbsp balsamic vinegar (I prefer 2, but perhaps start with 1)

salt and freshly ground black pepper

pinch of sugar

500 g ready-made gnocchi

2 Tbsp chopped fresh parsley, Parmesan shavings and lemon zest, for serving

WHAT TO DO

1. Heat the butter and olive oil in a frying pan over medium-high heat. When the butter starts to foam, add the mushrooms and cook for 3–5 minutes, or until they are just cooked through. Add the garlic and rosemary and cook for another minute.
2. Add the balsamic vinegar and leave to simmer for 3 minutes, or until the sauce starts to reduce and thicken slightly. Check for seasoning and add salt, pepper and sugar as you need to.
3. Meanwhile, cook the gnocchi in a large saucepan of salted boiling water for 1–2 minutes, or until the gnocchi pieces rise to the surface. Remove with a slotted spoon, place in a bowl, drizzle with a little olive oil and set aside.
4. To serve, divide the gnocchi between warmed snack-sized bowls, drizzle over a little extra olive oil, top with a spoonful of mushrooms and generous amounts of fresh parsley and Parmesan, and a scattering of lemon zest.

Notes: Add crispy bacon or chorizo bits for a meatier version. Adding crumbled feta or even Gorgonzola or goat's cheese just before serving would also be a delicious addition.
This recipe works well with penne or linguini too.

seafood.

HARISSA SQUID AND CHICKPEAS.

HARISSA IS ONE OF MY FAVOURITES FOR ADDING A LITTLE FIRE AND FLAMBOYANCY TO THE SIMPLEST DISHES, AND I LOVE THAT IT ADDS THAT LITTLE EXTRA NORTH-AFRICAN SOMETHING SPECIAL. I ALWAYS THINK THAT IT TASTES JUST A LITTLE LIKE FARAWAY PLACES SMELL. ADD TO THAT THE FACT THAT THIS CAN BE ON THE TABLE IN 15 MINUTES AND YOU'LL FIND IT'S FAIRLY SMASHING.

SERVES 4 | PREPARATION TIME 5 minutes | COOKING TIME 10 minutes

WHAT YOU'LL NEED

1 Tbsp olive oil
1 x 410 g can peeled, chopped tomatoes
1 tsp grated fresh ginger
1 clove garlic, crushed
½ tsp dried chilli flakes
½ tsp sugar
1–2 tsp harissa paste
400 g fresh squid or calamari
1 x 410 g can chickpeas, drained
salt and freshly ground black pepper
lemon juice, to taste
fresh coriander leaves, for garnishing

WHAT TO DO

1. Heat the olive oil in a heavy-based pan and add the tomatoes, ginger, garlic, chilli flakes, sugar and harissa paste. Cook for 1–2 minutes, or until the paste is fragrant.
2. Add the squid or calamari to the pan, place the lid on and leave to poach, turning halfway, for 8–10 minutes, or until it is white and cooked through.
3. Add the chickpeas and bring the sauce back up to a gentle bubble. Remove from the heat, add salt, pepper and lemon juice to taste. Garnish with fresh coriander leaves and serve immediately, either just as it is or with couscous or fresh crusty bread.

LEMONY HERBY HAKE
with Warm Baby Potato and Pea Salad.

I LOVE USING OUR SUSTAINABLE SOUTH AFRICAN HAKE FOR THIS RECIPE – IT'S A BRILLIANT BLANK CANVAS FOR SO MANY AMAZING FLAVOURS – BUT ANY OTHER SUSTAINABLE FIRM WHITE FISH WILL WORK HERE JUST AS WELL.

SERVES 4 | PREPARATION TIME 10 minutes | COOKING TIME 20 minutes

WHAT YOU'LL NEED

BABY POTATO AND PEA SALAD
400 g baby potatoes
1 cup frozen peas, thawed
small handful fresh mint leaves,
    roughly torn
1 Tbsp olive oil
salt and freshly ground black pepper

FISH
1 Tbsp olive oil
1 Tbsp butter
4 x 150–200 g hake fillets, skin on
    and scored (or any firm white sustain-
    able fish)
salt and freshly ground black pepper

LEMONY HERBY DRESSING
2 Tbsp lemon juice
3 Tbsp olive oil
1 tsp Dijon mustard
1 clove garlic, crushed
1 Tbsp chopped fresh parsley
1 Tbsp chopped fresh basil
1 tsp lemon zest

WHAT TO DO

1. First cook the baby potatoes for the salad. Boil them in a large saucepan of salted water until cooked through and they can be easily pierced with a knife, about 15 minutes.
2. Meanwhile, heat the olive oil and butter for the fish in a large saucepan over medium-high heat. Season the fish lightly with salt and pepper. When the butter starts to foam, add the fish and cook skin-side down for 3–4 minutes, or until the skin is crispy. Turn over and cook for 1–2 minutes on the other side, or until the fish is just cooked. Remove from the pan and set aside to rest.
3. Then make the lemony herby dressing by combining all the ingredients together in a clean old jam jar, and shake well until the mixture becomes 'creamy' and emulsifies. Check for seasoning and set aside. Pour half the dressing over the fish as it rests and while it is still warm; this way it will absorb more of the flavours.
4. Drain the potatoes and mix together with the remaining salad ingredients. Serve immediately with the fish and the remaining dressing on the side.

Notes: For a lighter version, serve this with a simple green salad on the side, reserving some of the dressing to toss through before serving, and top with a few Parmesan shavings.
You could also use 1 cup quinoa or couscous and cook according to packet instructions, then stir through the peas and mint along with a good drizzle of olive oil and lemon juice.

MUSSELS IN THAI RED CURRY.

DON'T YOU LOVE THE CLACKETY-CLACK THE CHAOTIC LITTLE TUMBLE MUSSELS DO AS YOU SEND THEM INTO THE POT? HERE THEY COME BACK TO YOU SWIMMING IN AN AROMATIC THAI SAUCE THAT'S REALLY RATHER WONDERFUL.

SERVES 4 | PREPARATION TIME 5–10 minutes | COOKING TIME 15 minutes

WHAT YOU'LL NEED

1 Tbsp olive oil
1 tsp grated fresh ginger
1–2 Tbsp Thai red curry paste
1 x 400 ml can coconut milk
1 cup good-quality fish or chicken stock
2 tsp fish sauce
1 tsp sugar
about 1 kg mussels in their shells, cleaned and de-bearded
handful fresh basil (or coriander), roughly chopped, for serving
lime wedges, for serving
fresh crusty bread, for serving

WHAT TO DO

1. Heat the olive oil in a medium-sized saucepan on medium-high heat, and cook the ginger and red curry paste until fragrant, 2–3 minutes. Add the coconut milk, stock, fish sauce and sugar and leave to simmer for about 5 minutes.

2. Just before serving, add the mussels to the saucepan, place the lid on and leave to cook for 3–4 minutes, or until the mussels have opened. Discard any that do not open at this stage.

3. Serve immediately in warmed serving bowls with a sprinkling of fresh basil or coriander and a squeeze of lime juice, as well as fresh crusty bread on the side. Also place empty bowls on the table for discarding the mussel shells.

QUICK FISHCAKES
with Summery Tomato and Avo Salsa.

THESE FISHCAKES ARE ABSOLUTELY ONE OF OUR FAVOURITE SUPPERTIME TREATS, ENDLESSLY SIMPLE AND HUMBLE BUT SO BEGUILING.

SERVES 4 | PREPARATION TIME 15 minutes | COOKING TIME 30 minutes

WHAT YOU'LL NEED

400 g firm white fish fillets, without skin

2 tsp olive oil

salt and freshly ground black pepper

3 medium-sized sweet potatoes

1 cup frozen peas

100 g feta cheese

1 Tbsp chopped fresh parsley

1 Tbsp chopped fresh mint or basil (optional)

1 Tbsp lemon juice

2 tsp lemon zest

1 egg, lightly beaten

SUMMERY TOMATO AND AVO SALSA

1 cup cherry tomatoes, halved

1 avocado, de-pipped, peeled and roughly chopped

2 Tbsp capers (optional)

1 Tbsp each of chopped fresh parsley and basil

½ fresh chilli, deseeded and finely chopped (optional)

1 Tbsp olive oil

1 Tbsp lemon juice

salt and freshly ground black pepper

100 g feta cheese, crumbled

WHAT TO DO

1. Preheat the oven to 200 °C.
2. Place the fish on the shiny side of a large sheet of tinfoil, drizzle with the olive oil and sprinkle with a pinch each of salt and pepper. Wrap up tightly and bake for 10–12 minutes, or until just cooked through, then remove and set aside to cool.
3. Meanwhile, halve and boil the sweet potatoes with their skins on for 15 minutes, or until soft, adding in the peas for the last 2 minutes of cooking time. Drain the sweet potatoes and peas, allow the potatoes to cool and steam for a few minutes and then remove the skins. Season with salt and pepper and mash roughly.
4. Flake the fish into a bowl, then add the mashed sweet potato and peas, feta, herbs, lemon juice, lemon zest and egg. Season with salt and black pepper and mix until combined.
5. Shape the mixture into 10–12 golf ball-sized patties, just gently flattened, and lay them in a lightly greased baking dish. Refrigerate for about 15 minutes to firm up a little, or until you are ready to cook.
6. In a preheated 220 °C oven, bake for 8–10 minutes, or until golden. If you'd like a crisper finish, then turn on the grill for the last 2–3 minutes.
7. Mix all the salsa ingredients together in a small bowl, sprinkling the feta on top, and serve on the side with the fishcakes.

PRAWN BUNNY CHOWS.

BUNNY CHOWS ARE AN ADORED STREET FOOD IN SOUTH AFRICA. A FRAGRANT SILKY CURRY IS SERVED IN HOLLOWED-OUT BREAD LOAVES FOR EASY TRANSPORTING, ALTHOUGH HERE I'VE SUGGESTED USING MINI PITA BREADS INSTEAD.

SERVES 8 as snacks or 4 as a main meal | PREPARATION TIME 15 minutes | COOKING TIME 30 minutes

WHAT YOU'LL NEED

1 Tbsp olive oil

1 Tbsp butter

½ tsp each of turmeric, medium-hot curry powder, ground coriander, ground cumin and dried chilli flakes

2 tsp freshly grated ginger

1 clove garlic, chopped

1 x 410 g can peeled, chopped tomatoes

1 tsp sugar

⅓ cup natural yoghurt

⅓ cup coconut milk

3 Tbsp ground almonds (not vital if you don't have)

500–600 g prawns, deveined and shelled

8–10 ready-made mini pita breads or mini bread loaves (topped and hollowed out to make space for the filling)

salt and freshly ground black pepper

handful chopped fresh coriander, for serving

lemon wedges, for serving

WHAT TO DO

1. Add the olive oil and butter to a medium-sized saucepan over medium-high heat. When the butter starts to foam, add the spices and fresh ginger and cook until fragrant, about 1 minute. Add the garlic and cook for another minute.
2. Add the canned tomatoes and sugar, turn the heat down to medium-low, and leave to simmer for about 15 minutes.
3. Add the yoghurt, coconut milk and ground almonds and stir to combine. Turn the heat back up to medium-high and add the prawns. Poach for 3–4 minutes in the curry sauce, or until cooked through and pink. Season to taste.
4. Spoon into the warmed pita breads or bunny chow bread loaves, and serve immediately with a scattering of fresh coriander and a squeeze of lemon juice.

Notes: This is a great 'make ahead' meal as you can cook the curry sauce up to a day in advance and then add the prawns shortly before serving.

Serve this with a cucumber, mint and mango salsa. Mix together ½ finely diced cucumber, 1 peeled and cubed fresh mango, ½ peeled and cubed fresh pineapple, 2 Tbsp chopped fresh mint, 1 deseeded and finely chopped fresh green chilli, 1 tsp grated fresh ginger, 1 Tbsp lime juice, 1 Tbsp honey and salt and freshly ground black pepper.

GRILLED TROUT
with Rainbow Salad and Asian Dressing.

THIS IS FRESH-FACED AND FABULOUS AND EVERYTHING YOU WANT FOR SUMMER FEASTING. IT'S ALSO AS PRETTY AS A PICTURE AND REMINDS ME OF SUMMERY, BREEZY DAYS IN THAILAND AND ALL THEIR CLEAN, LEAN, FRESH FOOD.

SERVES 4 | PREPARATION TIME 10 minutes | COOKING TIME 10 minutes

WHAT YOU'LL NEED

4 x 150 g trout fillets

2 Tbsp honey

4 Tbsp soy sauce

1 Tbsp grated fresh ginger

juice of 1 lime

RAINBOW SALAD

½ small red or white cabbage

1 small bulb fennel, stalks removed

2 medium-sized carrots

2 apples or pears, cored

1 red chilli, deseeded and sliced

handful fresh sprouts

handful salted peanuts

1 Tbsp each of chopped fresh mint
   and basil (or coriander)

ASIAN DRESSING

2 Tbsp grated fresh ginger

about ½ cup lime juice, or more
   to taste)

6 Tbsp honey

3 Tbsp soy sauce

2 Tbsp sesame oil

1–2 tsp fish sauce

WHAT TO DO

1. Preheat the oven to 220 °C.
2. Place the fish fillets in an ovenproof dish and drizzle over the honey, soy sauce and ginger. Cook for 8–10 minutes or until the fish is just cooked through and the flesh flakes easily with a fork.
3. While the fish cooks, prepare the salad ingredients by shredding in a food processor, then adding to a large serving bowl.
4. Mix all the dressing ingredients together and adjust according to taste. Pour the dressing over the salad and toss gently, making sure the salad ingredients are well coated.
5. Remove the fish from the oven and squeeze over the lime juice just before serving.

FISH BURGERS
with a Quick Wasabi Mayonnaise.

THE FLAVOURS IN THESE FISH BURGERS REMIND ME SO MUCH OF WHAT I LOVE ABOUT THE COLOURFUL CHAOS OF THE EAST, FULL OF FLAIR AND FEISTY FUN, ALL ROUNDED OFF NICELY WITH THE GOOD AND PROPER SMACK OF THE WASABI MAYO. YUM!

SERVES 4 | PREPARATION TIME 10 minutes | COOKING TIME 10–15 minutes

WHAT YOU'LL NEED
BURGERS
2 Tbsp soy sauce

1 tsp grated fresh ginger

1 Tbsp honey

juice of 1 lime, plus extra for serving

4 fish fillets, without skin (about 150 g
   each, and I prefer trout or salmon)

olive oil, for frying

4 fresh bread rolls, halved

1 avocado, de-pipped and thinly sliced

salt and freshly ground black pepper

fresh basil or coriander leaves, for
   garnishing

QUICK WASABI MAYONNAISE
1 egg

1 clove garlic

1/2 avocado, de-pipped and roughly
   chopped

2 Tbsp lime or lemon juice

pinch each of salt and freshly ground black
   pepper

1 tsp wasabi paste

3/4 cup cooking oil (not olive oil)

WHAT TO DO
1. Mix together the soy sauce, ginger, honey and lime juice to make a basting for the fish fillets. Spread over the fillets on both sides, then fry quickly in a hot pan with a little olive oil. Cook for 4–6 minutes, or until just cooked through and golden, turning halfway.
2. For the mayonnaise, add all the ingredients, except the oil, to a blender. Switch it on to a low speed and then slowly drizzle in the oil in a constant stream. Continue blending until all the oil is incorporated and the mixture thickens to the usual consistency of mayonnaise. Set aside.
3. To assemble the burgers: Remove the fish fillets from the pan once cooked and place onto the pre-cut bread rolls. Top with a dollop of the wasabi mayonnaise, a sliver or two of avocado, season with a little salt and pepper, and garnish with a small handful of fresh basil or coriander. Drizzle with an extra squeeze of lime juice and serve immediately.

Notes: If not using avocado in the mayonnaise, use 1 cup of oil.
The mayo makes 1 cup and keeps in the fridge for up to two weeks.

FIRESIDE FISH CURRY.

WHENEVER I THINK OF THIS RECIPE I THINK IMMEDIATELY OF THE NIGHT MARKET STALLS IN ZANZIBAR'S STONETOWN, BRIMMING WITH FAMILIES PREPARING FOOD TOGETHER TO SHARE AND SELL. IT'S A WONDERFULLY CHAOTIC ASSAULT ON THE SENSES: THE SMELL OF THE HARBOUR, THE ALL-ENCOMPASSING AROMA OF THE SPICES, THE DELICIOUSNESS OF THE SEAFOOD, THE CACOPHONY OF VENDORS AND SHOPPERS AND EATERS – IT MAKES FOR A VERY HAPPY PICTURE IN MY MIND'S EYE. IT WAS ALSO THE FIRST PLACE THAT I TASTED A KNOCK-YOUR-SOCKS-OFF SEAFOOD CURRY, AND FOR THAT I WILL ALWAYS BE VERY GRATEFUL.

SERVES 4 | PREPARATION TIME 15 minutes | COOKING TIME 25–30 minutes

WHAT YOU'LL NEED

1–2 Tbsp olive oil

1 medium-sized onion, chopped

1 tsp ground cumin

1 tsp dried coriander

1 tsp dried chilli flakes

1–2 tsp medium curry powder

½ cinnamon stick

3–4 cardamom pods, bruised to release the seeds

2 cloves garlic, chopped

1 thumb-sized piece of fresh ginger, peeled and roughly grated

1 x 410 g can peeled, chopped tomatoes

1 x 400 ml can coconut milk

2 tsp sugar, or to taste

salt and freshly ground black pepper

4 x 125 g fresh fish fillets, roughly chopped

2 Tbsp chopped fresh coriander, for garnishing

WHAT TO DO

1. Heat the olive oil in a large saucepan over medium-high heat. Add the onion, stir for about 2 minutes and then add the spices, garlic and ginger.
2. Stir for a further minute and then add the tomatoes. Reduce the heat and simmer for about 15 minutes, stirring often.
3. Add the coconut milk and sugar to the tomato mixture and check the seasoning. Add the fish, put on the lid and simmer for 5 minutes, or until the fish is just cooked through and can be flaked apart with a fork.
4. Check the seasoning again before serving with fresh naan breads or basmati rice, garnished with the fresh coriander.

HONEY AND SOY HAKE EN PAPILLOTE
with Pak Choi and Coconut Jasmine Rice.

THERE'S SOMETHING SPECIAL ABOUT TEARING OPEN A STEAMING PAPILLOTE BAG AND BEING ENVELOPED IN BEAUTIFUL, FRESH, CITRUSY ASIAN FLAVOURS (AND PS, PAPILLOTE IS JUST ANOTHER NAME FOR A PRETTY LITTLE PACKAGE MADE FROM BAKING PAPER THAT ALLOWS THE FISH TO STEAM UNTIL PERFECTLY FLAKY).

SERVES 4 | PREPARATION TIME 10 minutes | COOKING TIME 20 minutes

WHAT YOU'LL NEED

COCONUT JASMINE RICE
1 cup jasmine rice
1 cup coconut milk
1 cup boiling water

HAKE EN PAPILLOTE
800 g firm white sustainable fish fillets
salt and freshly ground black pepper
2 Tbsp soy sauce
2 Tbsp runny honey
2 tsp grated fresh ginger
2 Tbsp lime juice
1 red chilli, deseeded and finely chopped
handful fresh coriander, roughly chopped,
    for serving

PAK CHOI
1 Tbsp olive oil
2 heads baby pak choi, roughly sliced
    lengthways
1–2 tsp sesame oil
1 Tbsp soy sauce

WHAT TO DO

1. Preheat the oven to 200 °C.
2. Cook the jasmine rice in a mixture of the coconut milk and water, approximately 20 minutes. Keep an eye on it and add a little more water if you need to. Remove and set aside, toss with a fork and leave to steam gently.
3. Pat the hake fillets dry with kitchen paper, place onto a sheet of open baking paper (large enough to fully wrap the fish) and then season with salt and pepper. Coat with the remaining ingredients, except the fresh coriander.
4. To fold en papillotte do as follows: Place the two longer edges of the paper together, make a 1 cm fold, and then fold again until you have reached the fish fillet. Then repeat with the two remaining edges. Place in the oven and cook for 10–12 minutes, or until the flesh flakes apart easily with a knife.
5. Just before serving, heat the olive oil in a wok or pan and fry the pak choi along with the sesame oil and soy sauce.
6. Serve the fish and greens over the steaming jasmine rice and sprinkle with fresh coriander. Dress with extra lime juice and soy sauce, if necessary.

WHOLE SNOEK
with Apricot, Chilli and Ginger Glaze.

SNOEK IS A FAVOURITE FISH FOR THE BRAAI (BBQ) IN SOUTH AFRICA. IT'S SIMILAR TO MACKEREL AND IS SIMPLE, HONEST, COMFORT FOOD AT ITS BEST. THERE IS ALMOST ALWAYS APRICOT JAM INVOLVED SOMEHOW, AND HERE I'VE ADDED IN A KICK OF CHILLI AND A LITTLE STING OF GINGER TO JAZZ THINGS UP A BIT. I ORIGINALLY WROTE THIS RECIPE FOR MY TV SERIES *SARAH GRAHAM COOKS CAPE TOWN* WHEN WE COOKED THIS UP THE WEST COAST IN THE BEAUTIFUL SEASIDE TOWN OF SALDANHA.

SERVES 6 | PREPARATION TIME 10–15 minutes | COOKING TIME 15–20 minutes

WHAT YOU'LL NEED

1 fresh snoek, cleaned and prepared in 'butterfly' style

2 cloves garlic, grated

2–3 Tbsp olive oil, plus extra for greasing

1 red chilli, deseeded and finely chopped

2 heaped tsp grated fresh ginger

3 Tbsp apricot jam

1 Tbsp chutney

2 tsp soy sauce

3–4 sprigs fresh thyme

juice of 2 lemons

zest of 1 lemon

salt and freshly ground black pepper

2 Tbsp chopped fresh dill or parsley, for serving

WHAT TO DO

1. Prepare your braai or barbecue as you usually would for cooking, with low and gentle coals. Meanwhile, dry the snoek by blotting it very well with kitchen paper.

2. Mix together all of the remaining ingredients, which are for basting the snoek. Grease the skin side of the snoek with olive oil, and baste the inside with half of the glaze. Lay the snoek flat and skin-side down on the grid.

3. Braai the snoek for 10–15 minutes skin-side down, re-basting with the remaining glaze as you need to, and then about 5 minutes flesh-side down, with a further 2 minutes or so flesh-side up again, and at this point use up the remaining glaze. There is no need to baste the skin side. The fish is cooked when the flesh can be easily flaked apart with a fork.

4. Remove from the heat, leave to rest for a few minutes and then serve while still hot.

PRAWN RICE PAPER ROLLS.

THESE ARE GLORIOUSLY FRESH AND SUMMERY (ALMOST SMUGLY SO), AND FULL OF COLOUR AND CHARACTER – MY FAVOURITE FOOD FOR FEEDING FAMILY AND FRIENDS.

MAKES about 12 rolls | PREPARATION TIME 25 minutes | COOKING TIME 5 minutes

WHAT YOU'LL NEED

2 Tbsp olive oil

250–300 g prawns, deveined and shelled

1 cup mange tout or sugar snap peas, thinly sliced lengthways

1 red bell pepper, deseeded and thinly sliced lengthways

small handful fresh bean sprouts

2 Tbsp roughly chopped fresh coriander (or basil)

¼ cup roughly chopped roasted and salted peanuts (you could also use cashews)

10 sheets rice paper

PEANUT SESAME SAUCE

2 Tbsp sesame oil

1 large clove garlic, finely chopped

1 small chilli, deseeded and finely chopped (optional)

3 Tbsp soy sauce

6 Tbsp sweet chilli sauce

2 Tbsp smooth peanut butter

juice of 2 limes

WHAT TO DO

1. Heat the olive oil in a wok or large frying pan and fry the prawns until cooked through and just pink on all sides, about 5 minutes. Add the mange tout or sugar snap peas and red pepper for the last minute of cooking. Tip into a mixing bowl along with the sprouts, coriander or basil and nuts.

2. Combine all the sauce ingredients in a small bowl and pour a third over the prawns and vegetables. Toss gently to coat and allow to cool for a few minutes.

3. Ready a large bowl of warm water and have the rice-paper sheets laid out in front of you. One at a time, float the rice-paper sheets in the water for 30–45 seconds and remove just as they start to collapse and sink, but are still slightly 'al dente' as they will continue to soften after being removed from the water. (They look like sinking silk scarves when they reach this stage.) Lay them on a clean plate in front of you. Do not stack them, as they will stick together like glue.

4. To assemble the rolls, place about 2 Tbsp prawn mixture down the centre of each rice-paper sheet, then fold in the shorter edges and roll to close. Serve chilled or at room temperature with the extra sauce on the side.

Notes: These are equally delicious using chicken fillets/breast slivers or even firm white fish fillets.

If you don't have the time or can't find rice paper, cook rice noodles according to the packet instructions and serve as a meal for 2–3 people.

desserts.

PIMMS PLUMS AND PEACHES EN PAPILLOTE.

SERVES 4 | PREPARATION TIME 5 minutes | COOKING TIME 15–20 minutes

WHAT YOU'LL NEED

3 plums, stones removed and cut into
   thirds
4 peaches (or nectarines), stones removed
   and quartered, with peel intact
2 Tbsp Pimms (or brandy or fruit juice)
2 Tbsp honey
1 sprig fresh thyme (optional)
1 cinnamon stick
150 ml clotted cream or ice cream,
   for serving

YOU WILL ALSO NEED

4 sheets baking paper (about 30 cm
   in diameter)
baking tray

WHAT TO DO

1. Preheat the oven to 200 °C.
2. Prepare the plums and peaches or nectarines and toss together with the Pimms (or brandy or juice), honey, thyme and cinnamon in a mixing bowl. Leave to rest for 15 minutes if you have time.
3. Lay one sheet of baking paper onto a clean dinner plate and arrange 4 peach quarters and 3 plum pieces in the middle of the paper. Bring the long ends together and fold over neatly about three times to seal, then repeat with the short ends until you have a neat package. Place onto a baking tray and repeat with the remaining three sheets of baking paper.
4. Bake for 15–20 minutes, or until fragrant, and then serve immediately with a little clotted cream or ice cream. Serve the parcels on clean plates, leaving them closed until at the table.

Suggestion: Once you have opened the parcels at the table, add a handful of granola to each portion for an almost-instant fruit crumble.

HONEY-SPICED ROASTED FIGS
with Amaretti Crumble.

I SHARED THIS RECIPE IN MY FIRST TV SERIES, *SARAH GRAHAM COOKS CAPE TOWN*. I LOVE FIGS FOR THEIR EXOTICNESS AND ABILITY TO TRANSPORT OUR IMAGINATIONS TO FARAWAY PLACES. AND I LOVE HOW THEY SIT SO PRETTILY HERE, THEIR TOP HALVES CUT SO THAT THEY SEEM TO HAVE LITTLE 'ARMS' THAT REACH HEAVENWARD. THEIR CROWNING GLORY OF GOLDEN AMARETTI CRUMBS MAKES THEM EXTRA SPECIAL. DEFINITELY ONE OF MY FAVOURITES.

SERVES 8–10 | PREPARATION TIME 10 minutes | COOKING TIME 10–15 minutes

WHAT YOU'LL NEED

FIGS

10 fresh figs

3 Tbsp honey

¼ cup clementine or orange juice

1 cinnamon stick

1 star anise

mascarpone or vanilla ice cream, for serving

chopped fresh mint, for serving

AMARETTI CRUMBLE

1 heaped cup of Amaretti biscuits, crushed

2 Tbsp butter

2 Tbsp flour

2 Tbsp sugar

2 Tbsp toasted flaked almonds

WHAT TO DO

1. Preheat the oven to 220 °C
2. Gently cut across the crown of each fig, cutting two-thirds of the way down. Squeeze the base and the top should open like a flower. Place the figs into a shallow ovenproof dish.
3. Mix all the crumble ingredients together and add about 1 tsp to the top of each fig.
4. In a small saucepan, heat the honey, citrus juice, cinnamon stick and star anise until just before it simmers, then remove from the heat. Drizzle half the syrup over the figs and set aside the rest to drizzle over just before serving.
5. Roast the figs in the oven for 10–15 minutes, or until the crumble topping is golden, and the figs are cooked through and just starting to caramelise.
6. Serve with a drizzle of the remaining spiced honey, a dollop of mascarpone or vanilla ice cream and a sprinkling of chopped fresh mint.

NECTARINE TARTE TATIN.

IT'S BEST TO USE A CAST-IRON TARTE TATIN PAN IF AVAILABLE. IF NOT, THEN COOK OFF THE INGREDIENTS IN A REGULAR PAN AND TRANSFER TO A ROUND TART TIN JUST BEFORE BAKING.

SERVES 4–6 | PREPARATION TIME 15 minutes | COOKING TIME 30 minutes

WHAT YOU'LL NEED

2 Tbsp light brown sugar
2 Tbsp butter, at room temperature
1 tsp grated fresh ginger
1 vanilla pod, halved lengthways, or 1 tsp vanilla extract
1 cinnamon stick
5–6 nectarines (or peaches), peeled, stones removed and quartered (enough to cover the base of your pan)
1 sheet ready-made puff pastry, thawed (or enough to cover the nectarines in the pan)
1–2 tsp icing sugar, for serving
double-thick cream or vanilla ice cream, for serving

WHAT TO DO

1. Preheat the oven to 200 °C.
2. Add the sugar, butter, ginger, vanilla and cinnamon to the pan and cook over medium heat on the stovetop until the sugar has melted and started to turn a light golden brown colour, 3–4 minutes.
3. Remove the pan from the heat and carefully arrange the nectarines or peaches in the pan, as flat and close together as possible, so that the whole base is covered.
4. Meanwhile, cut out a circle of pastry that is just wider than the width of the pan. Lay the pastry over the nectarines or peaches, and tuck in the sides so that everything is well covered. (If you don't have an ovenproof pan, just transfer the nectarine mixture to a greased shallow ovenproof dish at this stage.)
5. Pierce the pastry a few times with a knife to allow steam to escape during cooking and bake for 25–30 minutes, or until the pastry is puffy and golden.
6. Leave the tart to cool for a few minutes before draining off any excess liquid and turning out onto a plate. Hold the plate over the pan with a dishcloth and invert the pan – be very careful, as the extremely hot caramel can spill out.
7. Discard the vanilla pod and cinnamon stick, sprinkle over a little icing sugar and serve immediately with cream or ice cream.

AMARULA MALVA PUDDING MUGS.

THIS IS MALVA PUDDING AT ITS VERY BEST. THE BODY OF THE PUDDING IS A PRETTY USUAL TAKE ON A VERY MUCH LOVED SOUTH AFRICAN FAVOURITE, BUT THE SAUCE IN THIS CASE HAS BEEN MADE INTO SOMETHING EVEN MORE GLORIOUS WITH THE ADDITION OF CONDENSED MILK, NUTMEG, A SMALL SPRINKLING OF ORANGE ZEST, AND CREAMY AMARULA LIQUEUR.

SERVES 8 | PREPARATION TIME 15 minutes | COOKING TIME 30 minutes
MAKES 8 small enamel mugs or 1 large pudding, about 20 x 20 cm

WHAT YOU'LL NEED

1 cup cake flour
1 tsp bicarbonate of soda
generous pinch of salt
1 egg
1 cup castor sugar
1 Tbsp apricot jam
2 tsp orange zest
1 Tbsp melted butter
1 tsp vinegar or lemon juice
1 cup milk
whipped or double cream, or vanilla
   custard, for serving

SAUCE

$\frac{1}{2}$ x 397 g can condensed milk
$\frac{1}{2}$ cup milk
$\frac{1}{2}$ cup fresh cream
$\frac{1}{4}$ cup Amarula liqueur (optional,
   alternatively use extra milk)
pinch of ground nutmeg
zest of 1 orange

WHAT TO DO

1. Preheat the oven to 180 °C and line a baking dish with baking paper, or grease eight enamel mugs.
2. Sift the flour, bicarbonate of soda and salt into a mixing bowl.
3. In a separate bowl, cream together the egg and castor sugar, and then add the apricot jam, orange zest, butter and vinegar or lemon juice.
4. Add the milk and the flour mixture to the egg mixture and beat well.
5. Pour into the baking dish or divide between the enamel mugs, cover with tinfoil and bake for 20–30 minutes, or until lightly golden and just cooked through (bake longer, until golden, if using one large dish).
6. To make the sauce, heat all the ingredients together in a medium-sized saucepan and pour over the puddings as soon as they come out of the oven, making holes in the surface of the puddings with a fork or skewer so that the sauce soaks in more easily.
7. Serve with whipped or double cream, or vanilla custard (or both!).

Note: You can make this pudding in advance and freeze it, thawing and reheating shortly before serving. You can also freeze leftovers for use at a later stage.

VETKOEKIES
with Spiced Chocolate Dipping Sauce.

OH GLORY. COULD THERE BE ANYTHING MORE ADORABLE THAN THE DEEP-FRIED DOUGHNUTTY LOVELINESS OF FLUFFY PILLOW-LIKE VETKOEKIES? IN SOUTH AFRICA THESE 'FAT CAKES' ARE MOST OFTEN SERVED WITH A DELICIOUSLY SPICY SAVOURY MINCE, BUT HERE I'VE DRESSED THEM UP IN A LITTLE GLOSSY MELTED CHOCOLATE.

MAKES about 20 | PREPARATION TIME 10 minutes | COOKING TIME 10–15 minutes

WHAT YOU'LL NEED

2 cups self-raising flour, sifted

1 tsp bicarbonate of soda

1 tsp salt

2 Tbsp sugar

2 eggs, beaten well

1 cup buttermilk

2 Tbsp milk

1 Tbsp melted butter

cooking oil, for deep-frying

SPICED CHOCOLATE DIPPING SAUCE

$\frac{1}{2}$ cup fresh cream

1 cinnamon stick

2 cardamom pods, bruised

$\frac{1}{2}$ cup chocolate hazelnut spread

CINNAMON SUGAR

4 Tbsp castor sugar

$\frac{1}{2}$ tsp ground cinnamon

WHAT TO DO

1. Sift the flour and bicarbonate of soda together into a large mixing bowl, then add the salt and sugar. Mix the wet ingredients together in a separate bowl, then pour into the dry ingredients and stir until you have a smooth batter. It will be quite thick.

2. Pour the oil into a large saucepan until it is about 4 cm deep, and heat. (If using a thermometer, the temperature of the oil should be 200 °C or a testing crumb should turn golden brown after 30 seconds.) Carefully drop in spoonfuls of the batter, 1 Tbsp at a time.

3. Fry until the vetkoekies are golden on all sides, turning them over from time to time. This will take 3–4 minutes. Drain on kitchen paper.

4. To make the sauce, heat the cream and spices in a small saucepan over medium heat until the cream reaches a gentle simmer. Strain and then whisk into the chocolate hazelnut spread until smooth and glossy. Loosen with a little hot water, 1 Tbsp at a time, if necessary.

5. Mix the castor sugar and cinnamon together and sprinkle over the vetkoek. Serve immediately with the chocolate dipping sauce.

BANANA PEANUT BUTTER ICE CREAM
with Cashew Nut Brittle.

THIS ALMOST-INSTANT ICE CREAM IS UTTERLY EFFORTLESS, AND TASTES LIKE THE SUM OF ITS SIMPLE PARTS, ONLY ABOUT A THOUSAND PERCENT BETTER. I'M PRETTY SURE THAT EVERY SPOONFUL OF SMOOTH, CREAMY, SOFT-SERVE TEXTURED BANANA-PEANUT-BUTTER GOODNESS WILL LEAVE YOU SWOONING.

SERVES 4 | PREPARATION TIME 30 minutes, plus 3 hours freezing time for the bananas

WHAT YOU'LL NEED

ICE CREAM

4 large ripe bananas, peeled and roughly chopped

2 Tbsp peanut butter (I use sugar-free)

2 Tbsp honey or maple syrup

2 Tbsp cold milk or natural yoghurt (or just water for dairy-free)

CASHEW NUT BRITTLE

100 g toasted cashew nuts (or other nuts of your choice)

3 Tbsp dark brown sugar

1 Tbsp butter

1 Tbsp maple syrup (or golden syrup if you don't have maple)

$1/2$ tsp ground cinnamon

WHAT TO DO

1. Place the bananas in a freezerproof container and freeze for at least 3 hours.
2. Meanwhile, prepare the nut brittle as follows: If the nuts are not toasted, toast in a heavy-based saucepan over medium heat until golden brown. Add the remaining ingredients, stir until well coated and then stir over medium-low heat for a further 5–10 minutes, or until the sugar has dissolved.
3. Remove the saucepan from the heat and pour the mixture onto a nonstick baking tray or silicone baking mat, then set aside to cool before breaking or chopping into rough pieces.
4. Once the banana pieces are frozen, place in a blender with the remaining ice cream ingredients and blitz until you have a smooth consistency. Serve immediately (soft serve style) with a scattering of nut brittle, or return to the freezer for 15–20 minutes to firm up a little more, if you prefer.

Note: For a healthier version, leave out the cashew nut brittle and just chop some toasted nuts and use those for your topping.

SPICED GUAVA CRUMBLE.

GROWING UP IN THE BUSH MEANT THAT FRESH FRUIT AND VEGETABLES WEREN'T ALWAYS THAT EASY TO COME BY, UNLESS WE'D GROWN THEM OURSELVES AND THEN OF COURSE OUR FAVOURITES WEREN'T ALWAYS IN SEASON. WE WERE TAUGHT NEVER TO TURN OUR NOSES UP AT A CANNED FRUIT DESSERT, AND BOY AM I GLAD ABOUT THAT. I LOVE FIGURING OUT NEW WAYS TO TURN SOMETHING SO SIMPLE INTO A PRETTY SPECIAL PUD.

SERVES 4–6 | PREPARATION TIME 10 minutes | BAKING TIME 10–15 minutes

WHAT YOU'LL NEED

SPICED GUAVAS
2 x 410 g cans guavas in syrup, drained and
   syrup reserved
1 cinnamon stick
1 star anise
1 vanilla pod, halved lengthways, or ½ tsp
   vanilla extract

CRUMBLE TOPPING
⅓ cup cold butter, cut into cubes
⅓ cup light brown sugar
½ cup cake flour
⅓ cup rolled oats
¼ cup chopped pecan nuts or almonds
½ tsp ground cinnamon
½ tsp ground ginger
thick cream, custard or vanilla ice cream,
   for serving

WHAT TO DO

1. Add the reserved guava syrup, spices and vanilla to a medium-sized saucepan over medium heat and simmer for 10 minutes, or until it reduces slightly and starts to thicken.
2. Meanwhile, preheat the oven to 200 °C. Mix together all the crumble ingredients until it has the consistency of coarse breadcrumbs.
3. Lay the guavas in a shallow ovenproof baking dish (or four to six individual ramekins). Scatter over the crumble topping and bake on the lowest shelf of the oven for 10 minutes, then turn on the grill and bake for a further 5 minutes, or until the crumble topping is golden. Serve immediately with thick cream, custard or vanilla ice cream, and a drizzle of the spiced syrup.

Note: For a camping-friendly version where no oven or grill is available, serve the poached guavas with a 'crumble' topping of healthy granola.

CINNAMON BAKED APPLES
with Almonds and Mascarpone.

WITH THESE GORGEOUS BAKED APPLES, THE CINNAMON COAXES EXTRA SWEETNESS OUT OF THE FRUIT, AND IT'S ALL BALANCED OFF BEAUTIFULLY WITH THE TOASTED BUTTERY NUTS AND SILKY MASCARPONE. WHAT'S NOT TO LOVE? YOU COULD ALSO USE PEARS, OR EVEN STONE FRUIT THAT YOU SIMPLY HALVE AND REMOVE THE STONE, SUCH AS NECTARINES, PLUMS OR PEACHES. BAKED FIGS ARE ANOTHER FIRM FAVOURITE OF MINE.

SERVES 4 | PREPARATION TIME 5 minutes | BAKING TIME approx. 25 minutes

WHAT YOU'LL NEED

2 Tbsp butter, at room temperature
handful chopped almonds or pecan nuts
pinch of ground cinnamon
4 apples, cored
1–2 Tbsp mascarpone or cream cheese
drizzle of fresh orange juice and grating of
    zest (optional)

WHAT TO DO

1. Preheat the oven to 180 °C and lightly grease a small baking dish.
2. Mix together the butter, nuts and cinnamon and divide the mixture between the apples, filling the holes where the cores were.
3. Place in the baking dish and bake for 25 minutes, or until golden and the apples are soft enough to eat easily with a fork. Add a little mascarpone or cream cheese to each apple and then drizzle over the orange juice and scatter over the zest just before serving for a little extra freshness.

Note: Speed up the process by boiling or microwaving the cored (but unfilled) apples for 4–5 minutes before filling them and placing them in the oven for 10–15 minutes, or until done to your liking.

SALTED CARAMEL AND FRIENDS.

SALTED CARAMEL IS HARDLY REVOLUTIONARY, AND I CERTAINLY CAN'T CLAIM IT AS MY OWN, THOUGH THIS RECIPE IS ONE THAT I HAVE POURED LOTS OF LOVE INTO PERFECTING, AND IT'S BECOME ONE OF MY VERY FAVOURITE KITCHEN QUICK-FIXES. IT'S EXQUISITE DRIZZLED SIMPLY OVER VANILLA ICE CREAM FOR A SPEEDY AFTER-SUPPER TREAT, BUT JUST AS LOVELY IN MY LITTLE BANOFFEE PUDDING POTS (POSSIBLY MY FAVOURITE PUD EVER), OR ADDING SILKY SWEETNESS TO BLISTERED PINEAPPLE SKEWERS. I ALSO LOVE TO GIVE IT AS A GIFT, ALL PRETTY IN A GLASS JAR WITH A LITTLE BOW.

MAKES approx. 2 cups | PREPARATION TIME 5 minutes | COOKING TIME 5–10 minutes

WHAT YOU'LL NEED

200 g castor sugar

1 Tbsp honey or golden syrup (helps to prevent crystals forming)

1 tsp butter

200 ml fresh cream

1 tsp sea salt flakes (or more to taste)

WHAT TO DO

1. Add the castor sugar and honey to a heavy-based saucepan over a medium-low heat, and cook until the sugar starts to melt. Gently swirl the pot from time to time to redistribute the heat and the melted sugar. Take care that the sugar doesn't burn, as this will affect the taste of your caramel. If the saucepan gets too hot, remove it from the heat from time to time.

2. Once all the sugar has melted, remove the pot from the heat and add in the butter and cream, whisking continuously as you do so. Take care as the mixture will bubble furiously as you add the butter and cream. Once everything has combined, return the saucepan to the heat for a minute or two, or until the sauce has thickened to your liking and is silky smooth. If there are any lumps at this stage, continue stirring over a low heat for a few minutes and most of them should dissolve. Any remaining lumps can be strained out before cooling.

3. Add in the salt 1 tsp at a time, according to your taste (be careful when tasting, the mixture will be extremely hot). Remove the saucepan from the heat, strain out any lumps that have not dissolved and leave to cool slightly before serving, or store in sterilised glass jars in the fridge for up to two weeks.

Salted Caramel Banoffee Pudding Pots

SERVES 4 | PREPARATION TIME 10 minutes (excluding caramel making)

WHAT YOU'LL NEED

8–10 digestive or ginger biscuits (or biscuits of your choice), roughly crushed

3–4 bananas, peeled and sliced

2 Tbsp salted caramel per person, warmed

200 ml fresh cream, whipped (or 4 Tbsp double-thick cream)

handful mixed toasted nuts, chopped

WHAT TO DO

1. Divide the crushed biscuits between four small glasses. Then layer in the bananas, caramel, whipped cream and toasted nuts.
2. Serve immediately with extra salted caramel on the side.

Blistered Pineapple Skewers with Salted Caramel Sauce

SERVES 4 | PREPARATION TIME 20 minutes (mostly unattended) | COOKING TIME 10 minutes

WHAT YOU'LL NEED

PINEAPPLE SKEWERS

8 bamboo skewers

1 ripe pineapple, peeled and cut into 2–3 cm cubes

1 tsp ground cinnamon

2–3 tsp light brown or demerara sugar

2 Tbsp salted caramel sauce per person, warmed

chopped fresh mint, for garnishing

WHAT TO DO

1. Soak the skewers in water for 10–15 minutes; this will save them from burning on the grill or over the coals. Thread the pineapple cubes onto the bamboo skewers.
2. Preheat your braai/BBQ. Sprinkle the cinnamon and sugar over the pineapple skewers and lay them down on the braai/BBQ grid (or in a hot griddle pan on your stove) and cook for 1–2 minutes on each side, or until just charred and blistered and golden.
3. Serve immediately with a drizzle of salted caramel sauce and a sprinkling of chopped fresh mint.

CINNAMON MILK TARTS IN A GLASS.

MILK TART IS A WELL-LOVED SOUTH AFRICAN DESSERT, KIND OF LIKE A SET CUSTARD THAT IS THICKENED WITH CORN-FLOUR. THERE ARE FEWER EGGS THAN IN A TRADITIONAL FRENCH-STYLE CUSTARD, SO MILK TARTS ARE GENERALLY A LITTLE LIGHTER, AND ARE USUALLY FLAVOURED WITH CINNAMON. TRADITIONALLY IT HAS A SHORT-CRUST PASTRY BASE, BUT IN THIS CASE I'M USING THE ALMOST-INSTANT VERSION OF CRUSHED GINGER BISCUITS, BECAUSE I'M GOING FOR CUTE LITTLE DECONSTRUCTED VERSIONS SERVED IN A GLASS.

SERVES 6 | PREPARATION TIME 20 minutes | COOLING TIME 30 minutes

WHAT YOU'LL NEED

BISCUIT BASE
12 ginger biscuits or digestive biscuits

3 Tbsp butter, melted

FILLING
800 ml full-cream milk

1 cinnamon stick or 1 tsp ground cinnamon

1 vanilla pod, halved lengthways

2 cardamom pods, bruised (gently squash
  them; they are optional)

2 eggs

$\frac{1}{2}$ cup sugar

$\frac{1}{4}$ cup cornflour

$\frac{1}{4}$ cup sifted cake flour

pinch of salt

1 Tbsp butter

1 tsp vanilla essence

1 tsp ground cinnamon and $\frac{1}{2}$ tsp ground
  nutmeg, for sprinkling

WHAT TO DO

1. To make the biscuit bases, blitz the biscuits in a food processor, or crush in a dishcloth using a rolling pin, then mix together with the melted butter until you have a beach-sand consistency.
2. Divide the biscuit mixture between six pudding glasses (something similar to martini glasses usually works well) or ramekins.
3. To make the filling, heat the milk in a saucepan, along with the cinnamon, vanilla and cardamom pods, until it just starts to boil, then remove from the heat.
4. In a heatproof bowl, beat the eggs well, and add the sugar, corn-flour, flour and salt. Mix well until combined and smooth.
5. Remove the cinnamon stick, cardamom and vanilla pod from the milk and slowly add the milk to the egg mixture. Return everything to the saucepan on a low heat and stir until the mixture reaches a thick custard-like consistency. This takes just a couple of minutes, so keep your eye on it; you don't want the mixture to burn.
6. Remove from the heat, add the butter and vanilla essence and stir.
7. Pour the mixture into the glasses/ramekins and leave to set at room temperature, or if you need to speed things up, in the fridge.
8. Sprinkle with cinnamon and nutmeg and refrigerate until ready to serve.

ESPRESSO PAVLOVA
with Spiced Poached Pears.

MY MUM IS A BIT OF A MERINGUE QUEEN. SHE USED TO CHURN OUT ARMIES OF THEM, AND WE'D HOLLOW OUT THE BOTTOMS, FILL THEM WITH WHIPPED CREAM AND STICK THEM BACK TOGETHER AGAIN. PRETTY LITTLE MERINGUE SANDWICHES. THIS PAVLOVA IS A NOD TO SO MANY SUNDAY LUNCHES AROUND VERY FULL AND MERRY TABLES, THOUGH I'VE ADDED A TWIST WITH THE ESPRESSO FLAVOURING AND BEAUTIFUL LAYER OF SPICY POACHED PEARS.

SERVES 8–10 | PREPARATION TIME 15 minutes | BAKING TIME 1 hour (mostly unattended)

WHAT YOU'LL NEED

PAVLOVA
6 large eggs, separated
300 g castor sugar
2 tsp instant espresso powder
2 tsp cornflour
1 tsp white vinegar or lemon juice

SPICED POACHED PEARS
200 ml water
100 ml apple or orange juice
zest of ½ orange
1 cinnamon stick
1 star anise
1 vanilla pod, halved lengthways
4 Tbsp light brown sugar or 3 Tbsp honey
3 firm pears, peeled, cored and cut
   into sixths

TO SERVE
1 cup fresh cream, whipped, or 1–2 cups
   double-thick Greek yoghurt
handful mixed nuts, toasted until golden
handful fresh mint leaves, to garnish

WHAT TO DO

1. Preheat the oven to 140 °C and line a baking tray with nonstick baking paper or a silicone mat.
2. Ensure the bowl of your electric mixer is clean and dry. Add the egg whites, and whisk until you have soft peaks. With the mixer running on medium speed, add the castor sugar in three to four stages, allowing the mixer to mix well in between, until the meringue is thick and smooth and can stand in firm peaks. Add the espresso powder, cornflour and vinegar and mix again until they are all incorporated.
3. Spread the mixture onto the baking tray in a circle, about 22 cm in diameter. Leave the outside edges slightly higher than the centre so that you have a gentle 'crater' shape to fill later. Bake for 20 minutes at 140 °C and then turn down to 120 °C and bake for another 45 minutes, or until the outside of the pavlova is dry to the touch. Switch the oven off, open the door slightly and leave the pavlova to cool completely. Store airtight until needed.
4. Meanwhile, add the poaching liquid and spices to a saucepan and bring to a simmer. Add the pears and simmer gently for 20 minutes, or until the pears are soft and can be easily pierced with a knife. Remove the pears and place in a bowl for later use, and reduce the poaching liquid for a further 10–15 minutes, or until syrupy.
5. To serve, top the pavlova with the whipped cream or yoghurt, pear slices, toasted nuts and a drizzle of the reduced poaching liquid. Garnish with fresh mint leaves and serve immediately.

CARAMELISED CARDAMOM BANANAS
with Coconut Cream.

CARDAMOM AGAIN. EVER SINCE I FIRST WENT TO EAST AFRICA I HAVE BEEN MILDLY OBSESSED WITH ITS ABILITY TO TRANSPORT ME SOMEWHERE EXOTIC. IT'S ALL ENCOMPASSING AND I LOVE IT, LIKE A BIG, WARM, SPICY HUG. HERE, I'VE USED IT TO ADD SOME SPECIAL FLAIR AND FLAVOUR TO A SIMPLE, SPEEDY AFTER-SUPPER TREAT.

SERVES 4 | PREPARATION TIME 5 minutes | COOKING TIME 5–10 minutes

WHAT YOU'LL NEED

3–4 ripe bananas

1 Tbsp butter

2 Tbsp dark brown sugar

3 cardamom pods, bruised until open and
   seeds removed

1 tsp vanilla extract

100 ml coconut cream

1 Tbsp honey

2 Tbsp slivered almonds, for serving

WHAT TO DO

1. Cut the bananas in half and then slice each portion in half lengthways.
2. Add the butter and sugar to a nonstick pan and when the butter starts to foam and the sugar has melted, add the bananas, cardamom seeds and vanilla and cook until the bananas are golden on both sides, about 4 minutes.
3. While the bananas cook, mix the coconut cream and honey together, and toast the almond slivers in a dry pan over medium heat.
4. Remove the bananas from the heat and serve immediately with a drizzle of the honeyed coconut cream and a scattering of toasted nuts.

ROSEWATER PANNA COTTA
with Sticky Raspberries and Honeyed Pistachio Nuts.

WHEN WE TRAVELLED TO TURKEY I COULDN'T GET ENOUGH OF THE GOLDEN, SYRUPY SWEET PISTACHIO-FILLED BAKLAVA THAT THEY SELL ON ALMOST EVERY STREET CORNER. THE HONEYED PISTACHIOS HERE ARE A LITTLE NOD TO THOSE SWEET MEMORIES; ALONG WITH THE ROSEWATER THEY LEND A LOVELY EXOTICNESS TO A SIMPLE PANNA COTTA, AND I LOVE BRINGING THOSE FLAVOURS BACK HOME TO MY KITCHEN.

SERVES 4 | PREPARATION TIME 10 minutes | COOLING TIME 3 hours

WHAT YOU'LL NEED

1 Tbsp castor sugar

400 ml fresh cream

100 ml full-cream milk

1 vanilla pod, halved lengthways and seeds scraped out

2 gelatine leaves

2 tsp rosewater (or try orange blossom)

TOPPING

1 cup fresh or frozen raspberries

1–2 Tbsp honey or castor sugar

2 Tbsp water

HONEYED PISTACHIO NUTS

$1/4$ cup runny honey

$1/3$ cup shelled and toasted pistachio nuts

WHAT TO DO

1. Place the castor sugar, cream, milk, vanilla seeds and vanilla pod into a small saucepan over medium heat, bring to a simmer and stir gently until the sugar dissolves, 2–3 minutes.

2. Meanwhile, soak the gelatine leaves in room temperature water until soft. Gently wring out any excess water from the gelatine, and add the gelatine to the vanilla cream mixture along with the rosewater. Stir until the gelatine has dissolved.

3. Divide the cream mixture among four ramekins and refrigerate for 2–3 hours or until set.

4. To make the topping, add the raspberries, honey or castor sugar and water to a small saucepan, mash the berries roughly with a fork and simmer for about 5 minutes, or until a little sticky. Remove from the heat and allow to cool slightly, then divide over the tops of the panna cottas.

5. For the honeyed nuts, warm the honey slightly and mix through the nuts, then use to garnish the desserts.

STEWED BERRIES
with Chai-spiced White Chocolate Cream.

A BOWL OF JEWEL-BRIGHT BERRIES IS LIKE SUMMER ON A PLATE. STEWED JUST LIGHTLY WITH A DASH OF LEMON JUICE AND ZEST, AND SERVED WITH A PUNCH OF FRESH ANISEED-Y BASIL MAKES IT A PUD TO BE PROUD OF, AND A DINNER PARTY DREAM. INSTEAD OF SUGAR, A DASH OF APPLE JUICE COUNTERACTS THE SHARPNESS OF THE LEMON AND THE BERRIES; A GREAT TIP FOR SUGAR-FREE FRUIT STEWING WHENEVER THE URGE STRIKES.

SERVES 4 | PREPARATION TIME 5 minutes | COOKING TIME 5 minutes

WHAT YOU'LL NEED

3 cups mixed fresh berries
1/3 cup apple juice
2 Tbsp water
juice and zest of 1/2 lemon or clementine

CHOCOLATE CREAM
100 ml fresh cream
1/2 vanilla pod or 1/2 tsp vanilla extract
1 star anise
1 cinnamon stick
zest of 1/2 clementine
100 g white chocolate, roughy chopped
fresh basil leaves or mint

WHAT TO DO

1. Add the berries, apple juice, water, citrus juice and zest to a saucepan on medium-high heat. Simmer for 3–4 minutes, or until the berries have just softened but still hold their shape. Remove from the heat and set aside.

2. Meanwhile, bring the cream, vanilla, spices and clementine zest to a gentle simmer. Remove from the heat and leave to steep for 5 minutes. Remove the whole spices and add the chocolate. Stir until the chocolate has melted and the mixture is silky smooth, returning to a low heat, if necessary.

3. Serve the berries immediately with a drizzle of the cream and a few fresh basil or mint leaves.

Notes: You could also use frozen berries, just stew for an extra minute. Make this using nectarines or any other stone fruit. Try adding in a little thyme if you do; it adds a lovely unique freshness.

MOCHA PISTACHIO AFFOGATOS.

IF I HAD TO SUM MYSELF UP IN JUST A FEW SHORT SENTENCES, ONE OF THEM WOULD BE THAT 'THE OTHER ME LIVES IN ITALY'. BESIDES THE FACT THAT I COULD LIVE HAPPILY ON PASTA FOR THE REST OF MY DAYS, IT'S PUNCTUATED BY THIS – HARDLY A RECIPE, MORE OF AN ASSEMBLAGE OF SORTS, BUT NONETHELESS A PERFECT PUD. COLD CREAMY ICE CREAM DROWNED IN WARM CHOCOLATEY COFFEE AND CROWNED WITH BEAUTIFUL EMERALD GREEN PISTACHIOS. SWOON.

SERVES 4 | PREPARATION TIME 10 minutes

WHAT YOU'LL NEED

150 ml good-quality filter coffee or
 espresso (must be hot)
1 Tbsp chocolate hazelnut spread
4 scoops vanilla or pistachio ice cream
2 Tbsp roughly chopped pistachios, toasted

WHAT TO DO

1. Just before serving, mix together the hot coffee and chocolate hazelnut spread until smooth.
2. Divide the ice cream between four small glasses, bowls or teacups.
3. Drizzle some of the sauce over each ball of ice cream and sprinkle over a few chopped pistachios before serving immediately. Alternatively, serve the sauce on the side and allow guests to pour their own at the table.

DARK CHOCOLATE TRUFFLES
with Pistachio Nut Dust.

MAKES approx. 20 truffles | PREPARATION TIME 15 minutes | COOLING TIME approx. 1 hour

WHAT YOU'LL NEED

200 g dark chocolate, roughly chopped into
    1 cm pieces
100 ml fresh cream, at room temperature
1 tsp butter
$\frac{1}{3}$ cup toasted pistachio nuts, finely
    chopped

WHAT TO DO

1. Melt the chocolate over a double boiler by 'nesting' a heatproof glass bowl over a saucepan of gently simmering water. Make sure the base of the bowl is not touching the water. When melted, stir in the cream and butter until smooth and glossy. OR, place the chocolate and cream into a heatproof bowl and microwave for 30-second bursts until melted (about 2–3 minutes), then stir in the butter until smooth and glossy. OR, place the chocolate in a heatproof bowl, bring the cream and butter to a gentle simmer and pour over the chocolate pieces. Leave to stand for 2–3 minutes, then stir gently with a spatula until the chocolate is melted, smooth and glossy.
2. Leave the mixture to cool to room temperature (about 1 hour, or speed up by placing the bowl in the fridge).
3. Line a baking tray with baking paper or a silicone baking mat. Pour the toasted pistachio nut crumbs onto a plate and spread out thinly.
4. Scoop out the chocolate mixture using a teaspoon or melon baller that has been dipped in hot water and then dried off, and roll into little truffles with cold hands. Then coat the truffles in the pistachio nut 'dust' by rolling gently in the crumbs, place carefully onto the baking tray and refrigerate until serving or packaging and gifting.

Note: To turn the truffles into hot chocolate, just before serving, add 1 cup milk per person, 1 halved vanilla pod, 1 cinnamon stick, 4 bruised cardamom pods, $\frac{1}{4}$ tsp ground nutmeg, 1 tsp honey per person and 1 heaped tsp espresso or instant coffee powder (optional) to a large heavy-based saucepan and bring to a simmer. While the milk heats up, place 3 truffles into a tall glass or mug for each guest, along with a teaspoon to stir as they go. Pour the hot milk over the truffles in each glass or mug and serve immediately.

PINK GIN FIZZ POPSICLES.

FUN, FUN, FUN. I HAVE WATCHED MANY SUNSETS OVER THE SAVANNA WITH A GIN AND TONIC IN HAND, AND I DON'T PLAN ON CHANGING THE HABIT ANYTIME SOON. INSTEAD, WE MIX IT UP A LITTLE BY ADDING IN OTHER BITS LIKE PRETTY PINK GRAPEFRUIT JUICE, AND THEN POP THEM INTO POPSICLE MOULDS FOR DELICIOUS FROZEN TREATS.

SERVES 4 | PREPARATION TIME 5 minutes | FREEZING TIME 3–4 hours

WHAT YOU'LL NEED
50 ml gin
200 ml fresh grapefruit juice
200 ml tonic
juice of 1 lime

WHAT TO DO
Mix all the ingredients together, adjust to taste and pour into popsicle moulds. Place in the freezer for at least 3 hours, or until firm.

baking.

QUICK THYME, FETA AND BLACK PEPPER MUFFINS.

ONE OF MY ALL-TIME AFTERNOON FAVOURITES ARE MY MUM'S CHEESE 'SCONES' (ACTUALLY THEY'RE MORE LIKE LIGHT AND FLUFFY MUFFINS). ROB'S BEEN KNOWN TO MAKE SHORT WORK OF AN EMBARRASSING AMOUNT OF THEM IN ONE SITTING. BESIDES THEIR SIMPLE DELICIOUSNESS, THEY CAN BE THROWN TOGETHER IN MINUTES. THIS VERSION INCLUDES FETA AND THYME, WHICH ADDS A LITTLE EXTRA SOMETHING.

MAKES 6 regular-sized muffins | PREPARATION TIME 5–10 minutes | BAKING TIME 15 minutes

WHAT YOU'LL NEED
1 cup self-raising flour, sifted
⅔ cup grated Cheddar cheese
⅓ cup crumbled feta cheese
½ tsp salt
½ tsp freshly ground black pepper
1 tsp baking powder
½ tsp Dijon mustard
½ tsp dried thyme
1 cup milk
cold butter, for serving

WHAT TO DO
1. Preheat the oven to 200 °C and lightly grease a muffin tray.
2. Combine all of the ingredients, except the milk and butter, in a large mixing bowl. Then add the milk, mixing everything together gently until all of the ingredients are just incorporated.
3. Spoon into the muffin tray and bake for 15 minutes, or until golden and puffy.
4. Remove from the tray and allow to cool slightly before halving the scones. Serve each one with a generous scraping of cold butter.

LEMONY SCONES
with Berry and Thyme Jam.

IF YOU'VE BEEN FOR TEA AT MY HOUSE, CHANCES ARE THAT YOU'VE HAD A VERSION OF THESE (AND YOU'LL ALSO KNOW HOW MUCH I LOVE AFTERNOON TEA). I MIX IT UP ALL THE TIME, AND ADD IN BERRIES, CHUNKS OF DRIED APRICOTS, EVEN CINNAMON. HERE, WITH JUST A HINT OF LEMON, THEY ARE EXQUISITE IN THEIR SIMPLICITY. THERE IS ALSO NO DRAMA OF ROLLING AND CUTTING OUT YOUR SCONES, THE MIXTURE FALLS RIGHT OFF THE SPOON ONTO YOUR BAKING TRAY FOR A FUSS-FREE TEATIME TREAT IN MINUTES. THE REST OF THE TIME IS THEN LENT TO FOOT TAPPING AS YOU WATCH THEM TURN FROM CREAMY COLOURED TO LIGHT GOLDEN BROWN WHILE THEY BAKE. OR, IF YOU'D LIKE TO BE A REAL SMARTY-PANTS, MAKE MY QUICK BERRY AND THYME JAM WHILE YOU WAIT (SEE OPPOSITE).

MAKES 12 | PREPARATION TIME 10–12 minutes | BAKING TIME 15 minutes

---

WHAT YOU'LL NEED

100 g castor sugar or light brown sugar
100 g unsalted butter
1 Tbsp lemon zest
1 large egg
1 large egg yolk
1 cup natural yoghurt
300 g cake flour, sifted
2 tsp baking powder
1 tsp bicarbonate of soda
½ tsp salt
butter, jam and clotted or whipped cream,
    for serving

WHAT TO DO

1. Preheat the oven to 180 °C and lightly grease two nonstick baking trays.
2. Mix all of the ingredients together until well combined (I usually use my food processor).
3. 'Drop' dollops of the mixture onto the baking trays using two table-spoons, leaving about 3 cm in between each scone (I usually put 6 scones on each baking tray).
4. Bake for 15 minutes or until lightly golden and a skewer inserted into the centre of a scone comes out clean.
5. Serve fresh from the oven with butter, jam and whipped cream.

Note: I often only cook half the scones and place the other tray straight into the freezer for easy baking another time. You can then bake them straight from frozen, just increase the baking time by 2–3 minutes.

Quick Berry and Thyme Jam.

THIS IS TECHNICALLY MORE A 'STEWED FRUIT' THAN A JAM, BUT IT MAKES BEAUTIFUL FRIENDS WITH THESE SCONES, AND IS ALSO AT HOME NESTLED AMONGST SOME DOUBLE-THICK GREEK YOGHURT FOR A SPEEDY BREAKFAST TREAT.

MAKES 3 x 250 ml jars | PREPARATION TIME 5 minutes | COOKING TIME approx. 30 minutes

WHAT YOU'LL NEED

500 g mixed fresh berries
¼ cup runny honey
1 vanilla pod
2 Tbsp orange juice
3 sprigs fresh thyme or 1 tsp dried
    (optional)
2 tsp orange or lemon zest (optional)

WHAT TO DO

1. Add all of the ingredients, except the zest, to a large heavy-based saucepan and stir over medium heat until the honey has warmed through and mixed with the rest of the ingredients.
2. Turn the heat up and bring the mixture to a vigorous boil, stirring occasionally, then turn the heat down to medium-low and leave to simmer for 15 minutes, or until the mixture thickens slightly and the fruit starts to break down and the syrup coats the back of a wooden spoon.
3. Remove the saucepan from the heat, stir through the zest (if using), leave the jam to cool slightly, then pour into sterilised jars and seal. Refrigerate after opening and use within two weeks.

CHOCOLATE CHIP FUDGE.

GROWING UP, I SPENT COUNTLESS HOURS AT THE STOVE STIRRING AND COAXING SUGARY SWEETNESS TO FUDGY GLORY. TIME WELL SPENT, SURELY? EVERYONE NEEDS THIS IN THEIR ARSENAL.

MAKES a 20 x 20 cm baking tray of fudge or approx. 16 large squares | PREPARATION TIME 5–10 minutes | COOKING TIME approx. 30 minutes (excludes setting time)

WHAT YOU'LL NEED
400 g light brown sugar
150 ml milk
2 Tbsp butter
1 Tbsp golden syrup
1 x 397 g can condensed milk
1 tsp vanilla essence
⅔ cup chocolate chips
pinch of salt

WHAT TO DO
1. Lightly grease a baking tray. Add the sugar and milk to a large, heavy-based saucepan over a low heat. Stir until the sugar has dissolved.
2. Add the butter and syrup and stir until the butter has melted.
3. Add the condensed milk and stir until the mixture starts to boil. Turn the heat down to medium-low and continue to simmer, stirring often, until the mixture darkens and takes on a golden caramel colour (soft ball stage). You will start to see sugary 'spiderwebs' on the inside of the saucepan as you stir; this means it is nearly ready. (Note: the fudge mixture will be extremely hot at this stage.)
4. Remove the saucepan from the heat, add the vanilla, half the chocolate chips and a pinch of salt, then stir vigorously using a wooden spoon for about 5 minutes; this will give you really smooth, glossy fudge. As the mixture cools it will start to thicken.
5. Pour into the prepared baking tray, sprinkle over the remaining chocolate chips, and leave to cool. Then cut into squares using a sharp knife. Store in an airtight container in the fridge or freezer.

ROSEMARY SHORTBREAD.

SURELY MY ZIMBABWEAN GRANNY JINTY MADE THE BEST SHORTBREAD IN THE HISTORY OF THE WORLD, EVER? WELL, WE LIKE TO THINK SO. UNFORTUNATELY, I CAN'T FIND HER EXACT RECIPE, BUT THIS ONE CONJURES UP A LOT OF THE BUTTERY LOVELINESS THAT I REMEMBER, AND I LOVE THE DELICATE UNDERTONES OF ROSEMARY. DUNK IT IN FRESH LEMON OR GRAPEFRUIT CURD, OR ADD A DRIZZLE OF MELTED WHITE CHOCOLATE AND IT'S MAGICAL.

MAKES 10 slices | PREPARATION TIME 35 minutes (including resting time) | BAKING TIME 25–30 minutes

WHAT YOU'LL NEED

125 g butter, at room temperature

60 g icing sugar or castor sugar

1 tsp finely chopped fresh rosemary

125 g cake flour

60 g cornflour

pinch of salt

2 Tbsp castor sugar

WHAT TO DO

1. Cream the butter, icing sugar and rosemary together using an electric mixer or in a large mixing bowl using a wooden spoon.
2. Sift the cake flour, cornflour and salt into the mixture and mix using a wooden spoon or the paddle attachment on your mixer, until the mixture has the consistency of breadcrumbs. Scrape down the sides of the bowl as you go along to make sure it is all well incorporated.
3. Gently bring the mixture together into a ball using your hands.
4. Roll the dough out until it's approximately 5 mm thick and cut out into heart shapes. Alternatively, press the mixture directly into a square or round cake tin that has been lined with baking paper, and smooth out the dough using the back of a tablespoon.
5. Pierce each section two to three times with a fork. Sprinkle over 1 Tbsp of the castor sugar and chill for 15–30 minutes.
6. Preheat the oven to 170 °C and bake for 25–30 minutes, or until lightly golden. Cut into slices or squares while still warm, sprinkle with the remaining castor sugar and then leave to cool on a wire rack.

EASY ESPRESSO CAKE
with Mocha Buttercream.

THIS CAKE IS JUST A LITTLE BIT GROWN UP AND FANCIFUL WITH ITS ESPRESSO THIS AND MOCHA THAT, BUT ANY COMPLICATIONS END RIGHT THERE. IT'S SUPER SIMPLE TO MAKE AND IS A VERY BEGUILING CROWD PLEASER.

SERVES 8–10 | PREPARATION TIME 15 minutes | BAKING TIME 25 minutes

WHAT YOU'LL NEED

200 g butter
200 g castor sugar
200 g self-raising flour
1 tsp baking powder
pinch of salt
4 large eggs
2 tsp instant coffee granules, dissolved in
   1 Tbsp hot water

MOCHA BUTTERCREAM

150 g butter, at room temperature
300 g icing sugar
1–2 tsp instant coffee granules and 2 tsp
   cocoa dissolved in 3 Tbsp warm milk

OPTIONAL

10–12 toasted and roughly chopped
   walnuts or pecan nuts, for decorating

WHAT TO DO

1. Preheat the oven to 190 °C and grease and line two 20 cm cake tins.
2. Cream together the butter and castor sugar for 3–5 minutes until the mixture is light and fluffy. As you go along, scrape down the sides of the mixing bowl with a spatula, as needed.
3. Sift together the flour, baking powder and salt into a clean bowl.
4. Add the eggs to the butter and sugar mixture, alternating with the flour mixture in between each addition. This will ensure that the eggs don't curdle and that your flour is well incorporated. Add the coffee mixture and mix a little more until everything has blended together.
5. Divide the batter between the two cake tins and bake for 25 minutes, or until golden and a skewer inserted into the centre comes out clean, or the cake springs back when pressed gently. Leave the cakes to cool in the tins for about a minute, then run a spatula around the inside edge and turn the cakes out onto a wire cooling rack.
6. To make the buttercream, cream together all the ingredients, adding extra coffee or cocoa to your liking. Once the cakes have cooled completely, top one cake half with half the icing, place the second cake half gently on top and add the remaining icing, followed by the toasted nuts, if you choose to use any.

ORANGE AND THYME YOGHURT LOAF CAKE.

I LOVE THIS CAKE. IT'S EASY TO MAKE AND UTTERLY UNASSUMING, WHAT WITH IT'S SOMEWHAT UNGAINLY LOAF SHAPE, BUT IT NEVER FAILS TO PLEASE. HERE THE ORANGE AND THYME LIFT IT JUST A LITTLE TO LOFTIER HEIGHTS.

SERVES 6–8 (MAKES 1 medium-large loaf tin) | PREPARATION TIME 10 minutes | BAKING TIME 35–40 minutes

WHAT YOU'LL NEED

125 g butter, at room temperature
2 heaped tsp orange zest
1 tsp dried thyme
1 cup castor sugar
3 eggs
2 cups self-raising flour, sifted
1/2 cup natural yoghurt or buttermilk

ORANGE AND THYME SYRUP
juice of 2 oranges (or equivalent to 1/2 cup)
2 Tbsp lemon juice
1 tsp grated fresh ginger (optional)
1 sprig fresh thyme or 1/2 tsp dried
1/4 cup water
2 Tbsp castor sugar or 2 Tbsp honey

WHAT TO DO

1. Preheat the oven to 180 °C. Grease a medium-large loaf tin and dust lightly with flour to make absolutely sure the cake won't stick.
2. Cream together the butter, zest and thyme, and gradually add the castor sugar until the mixture is thick and creamy, 3–4 minutes.
3. Add in the eggs, one at a time, and then fold in the flour and yoghurt.
4. Pour the batter into the loaf tin and bake for 35–40 minutes, or until golden and a skewer inserted into the centre comes out clean. Remove from the oven, prick holes in the top and allow to cool for a few minutes while you make the syrup.
5. To make the syrup, simmer all the ingredients together in a small saucepan until the sugar has dissolved, and then bring to a boil for 2–3 minutes without stirring or until it thickens slightly. Allow to cool slightly then pour over the warm cake and serve.

MY FAVOURITE CHOCOLATE TRAY BAKE
with Chocolate Peanut Butter Frosting.

WE HAVE THE LOVELIEST LITTLE PARK WHERE WE LIVE, AND SOPHIE AND ISLA ESPECIALLY LOVE AN AFTERNOON BASKING IN THE SUNSHINE AND RUNNING WILD WITH THEIR LITTLE POSSE OF PALS. IF EVER WE NEED AN ALMOST-INSTANT CAKE TO TAKE ALONG WITH OUR FLASK OF TEA, THIS IS IT. SOMETIMES IT GETS A LITTLE CROWNING OF SMARTIES OR OTHER COLOURFUL SWEETS, BUT EVEN BARE-FACED ITS SQUIDGY CHOCOLATINESS IS GREEDILY GOBBLED WITHIN MINUTES. IT'S ALSO ONE OF THE MOST FORGIVING CAKE RECIPES I KNOW.

SERVES 8 | PREPARATION TIME 10 minutes | BAKING TIME 20–25 minutes

WHAT YOU'LL NEED

1 cup sugar

1 cup cake flour, sifted

¾ tsp baking powder

¾ tsp bicarbonate of soda

3 Tbsp cocoa powder

1 heaped tsp instant coffee granules (optional)

pinch of salt

2 eggs

½ cup milk

1 Tbsp cooking oil

1 tsp vanilla essence

½ cup boiling water

CHOCOLATE PEANUT BUTTER FROSTING

2–3 heaped Tbsp smooth peanut butter

2–3 heaped Tbsp chocolate hazelnut spread

3–4 Tbsp boiling water

WHAT TO DO

1. Preheat the oven to 180 °C and grease your favourite cake tin or roasting tin (I like to use an old battered 15 x 20 cm roasting tin and then just serve the cake straight from that for a rustic effect).
2. Add all of the cake ingredients, except the boiling water, to a large mixing bowl.
3. Slowly add the boiling water, whisking as you pour it in, and mix until everything is just combined.
4. Pour into the cake tin and bake for 20–25 minutes, or until just cooked through and a skewer inserted into its centre comes out clean.
5. To make the frosting, whisk the ingredients together until smooth, altering the quantities to suit your preferred consistency and taste.
6. Ice the cake and serve as soon as possible.

Notes: Because I serve my cake in the tray that I bake it in, I only need enough icing for the top. If you decide to bake your cake in a cake tin and remove it and ice properly, you will probably need about double the amount of icing that is given above.

I like to add all of the dry ingredients to a glass jar and store in my pantry, that way it's extra quick to throw together when we need to, just add the wet ingredients at the last minute.

This also makes a pretty lovely little pud, served warm and with a generous scoop of vanilla ice cream or double-thick cream.

INDEX